POWERFUL WORDS

Dawn of a Profession

The New Way to Sell Financial Advice

DANI PEER

Published by Palmer Higgs Pty Ltd

First published 2014

© 2014 Dani Peer

The moral right of the author has been asserted.
A Cataloguing-in-Publication record is available from the
National Library of Australia.
ISBN: 978 0 992 54939 8 (pbk)
        978 0 992 54940 4 (ebk–ePub)

Designed, typeset and printed by Palmer Higgs
palmerhiggs.com.au

Distributed by Dennis Jones and Associates
dennisjones.com.au

To my treasured family.

To all those who've shared my journey.

To financial advisors everywhere who've given their clients a better life.

Contents

"Words are the currency of productivity. The words you use will ultimately determine the fate of your business."

Dennis Ross III – Ghost writer

Introduction: A crucial capability that few have mastered

My late father Shlomo made his mark on the South African life insurance industry in the early seventies. As a boy I grew up with words such as lapses, underwriting, whole life policies, clients, claims and rate books; and the people who used these. I watched how the insurance and nascent advice industry morphed with the changing times from the front row. How consumers' needs changed, how the products and services reshaped themselves to meet these needs. From my row I got to see and often meet the giants of the industry, the most successful agents and brokers, those continuously courted by the big companies.

Each year my father would throw a Gatsby-type party at our house. Shultz, the caterer, would industrialise our kitchen. Like a sushi train, his team of well-drilled waiters would rotate in and out with greasy and delicious food. I can still remember the meaty, smoky smell of sizzling cocktail sausages, each speared with a toothpick and packed tight on serving plates. Waiters bopped and weaved their way through a dense crowd of company folk (and their partners): senior executives, high-powered actuaries, fund managers, the marketing gurus, the less glamorous from administration and, of course, the sales stars. Drink in one hand, finger food in the other, the conversations were loud and passionate. It was a comfortably warm night in a leafy suburb of Johannesburg many, many years ago …

I had a special part to play at this celebration of the insurers. I had an unusual hobby – I played the bagpipes. My father called for silence (not so easy over a few hundred conversations). The food train briefly paused, voices trailed off and I pumped my bag with air …

Those days are long gone. I lost my dad in early 2000 and immigrated with my family to Australia later that year. But in some ways, those days are still with me right now. After a short, post-university journey in the accounting profession, I unsurprisingly discovered that the fire initiated by my boyhood experiences still burned. I practised for several years as a financial advisor before becoming fascinated with the business of financial advice. It's akin to finding more joy working on your business than in your business.

For the last twelve years I have worked with large institutions, mid-sized financial advisor dealer groups and individual advisors to build better businesses.

And in every one of my engagements I'm reminded that success does not come from fancy offices, power dressing, or a well-known brand. It does not come from the technology used or the fluency of the processes around which the business is built. It does not come from colourful marketing material or high-quality documentation. All these factors are important, but play a minor role. The key ingredient to success in this profession is the capability of the advisor. Financial advice is the ultimate people's business, where people are the assets of the business as well as its consumers.

The successful financial advisor must master two types of capability – technical and enabling. And it's the latter that really counts.

Technical capability includes all the hard content a financial advisor must master. Examples would include the ability to deliver relevant solutions to client needs, product features and benefits, and the ability to operate the technology used to drive the advice process and support the business. This content is made up of facts available in text books and user manuals.

Technical capability is the ticket to the game. Most advisors will have some degree of proficiency here. In many countries most of this knowledge is a legal requirement. You cannot operate as a financial advisor without a licence and, in order to receive this, you need certain qualifications. You cannot sell a product unless you are accredited to do so via an assessment.

Enabling capability is required to commercialise the advisor's technical skill sets. Unlike most other professions, financial advice needs to be sold. Sick people seek out doctors, those needing to submit their tax return bang on the door of the accountant. You want to build a house? Chase down an architect. Someone threatening to sue you or you just need some mundane contract drafted? Find a good lawyer. No one wakes up saying, "Damn, I may be underinsured. Better do something about that, and quick." Few, at least until it's too late, mutter on their drive in to work, "I wonder if I'm anywhere close to being on track to retire one day."

Such is the life of the financial advisor. Success in our profession demands that we mobilise people. Our fight to do this is on several fronts. It's not just against the natural and universal forces of apathy and procrastination. Other headwinds include the jaded reputation our industry has acquired by being too closely associated with product distribution rather than the provision of advice. There's also the challenge of selling something intangible, the benefits of which may not be apparent for many years. Add to this mix the complexity of advice coupled with the lack of financial knowledge of the average client. Finally, while financial advice itself is made up of logical and structured strategies, the assumptions behind the modelling of each strategy are just that – assumptions. We work in a field of uncertainty. We don't know where financial markets are heading, or what the inflation rate will be in a few years. Exchange rates? Interest rates? Even how long each of our retiree clients will live is unknown. Somehow our market devalues what we have to offer simply because our service comes with no guarantees. And to top everything, our profession receives regular broadsides from both the media and government, the latter who seem to think that our craft can somehow be regulated into certainty.

Enabling capability allows the advisor to rise above these obstacles. To create and maintain a profitable and enjoyable business. A successful business. While technical capability is the skill set that empowers you to advise, enabling capability is the skill set that motivates your clients to listen to and action that advice. Enabling capability is much more than sales skills. It's an understanding of buying psychology, the crafting of a compelling conversation, and the ability to get your client completely engaged in what you're saying. It's the skill required to compose questions that get clients to say, "Wow, I've never thought of it in that way." Enabling skills include an understanding of persuasive psychology and an ability to put this into practice when such leverage is required. Enabling skills equip you to articulate the value you bring to a relationship not as a corny sound bite, but in a way that allows the client to find the peculiar value they seek.

The ability to provide valuable advice is simply the key to this profession. The ability to motivate your market to choose to do business with you and to pay a fair and commercial fee will determine the level of success you experience as a financial advisor.

Powerful Words is a collection of the best thinking I have encountered on the topic of enabling skills. It will provide you with practical, easy-to-master capabilities that are the cornerstone of the most successful advisors. The material in this book has been sourced from within and outside our profession. The insights, tips, tactics, philosophies, formulae, questions and other content have been tested in the marketplace. And I've had the pleasure of witnessing their profound and positive impact for over a decade.

Final word. This is a book for busy people. While I haven't dumbed down any content, I have condensed my writing to essential elements only. Please accept this as an invitation to dig deeper if desired.

DANI PEER

Melbourne July 2014

Chapter 1:

Cognitive mapping – a peek into our buyer's mind

"Satisfying the listener at each stage of the thinking process enables him or her to buy rather than feel that they have been sold an idea, service or product."

Tom Lambert
The Power of Influence

My brother-in-law Michael sounded very excited. He'd just discovered an online "university" that allowed you to design your own syllabus. And what's more, there were no exams. Students were only required to write essays to prove their knowledge and competence. Both Michael and I are compulsive learners, so I was curious to see what he'd got involved in. And so I was rewarded with a most valuable and insightful mentoring relationship.

The discovery wasn't so much a university as an opportunity for those seeking particular knowledge to pair with someone who was able to provide it. From the website it appeared that the providers (the "faculty") were very accomplished practitioners, many of whom had published several books in their respective fields. The wrinkle in this business model occurred when its creators cheekily called themselves a university, provoking an online furore from the formal academic community. The words "scam" and "diploma mill" kept appearing in my Google searches. I reckon that an important part of the value of any degree lies in the credibility of the issuing institution. These guys had shot themselves in the foot – their concept was great, their credibility severely impaired. However, I wasn't looking for a qualification, but a wise guide. I read through the resume of each faculty member and soon found a person with just the credentials and experience I was looking for in the form of Professor Tom Lambert.

Lambert's speciality was consulting. His books *High Income Consulting* and *High Value Consulting* are considered major works in the field of business consulting. However, it was because of his allied interest in the field of influence and the use of psychology as a sales tool for professional service providers that I wanted to work with him.

What he taught me was pure gold. And I want to share this with you …

Cognitive psychology and reading your client's mind

Professor Lambert provided me with a sales framework he developed from his research into cognitive psychology. Cognitive psychology is the study of how people think. Almost everything we do is the result of a thought process, which often takes place on a subconscious level. Cognitive psychology, when applied to persuasion, influence and the challenge of selling financial advice is particularly useful. It provides us with a map for our client conversations that empowers us to understand how the conversation needs to flow in order to arrive at the point where a client says, "Yes, I would like to work with you."

Equally useful is the opportunity to understand where our client is on the buying journey. With a bit of practice you'll be able to pick out the stage of the buying process your client's mind has reached. This capability ensures that you direct your conversation and fine-tune your words in a way that responds to what your client seeks rather than the script or pitch you'd like to communicate. I have used the cognitive map as a framework on which to attach the various enabling skills discussed in the rest of this book. So don't stress if you aren't comfortable with the speed at which I'll take you through the map in this chapter. There will be frequent references to these concepts in later chapters.

Lambert describes the cognitive map as enabling us to "look into the client's mind and see what they are thinking as they make the buying decision".[1] To me this is the neatest and most elegant approach to getting your client to buy, rather than you having to sell. It maintains the gravitas of the professional advisor. If you can understand what your client is thinking, then you can respond accordingly. Lambert succinctly captures the value of this philosophy when he says, "By labelling thoughts in the order that they occur with the statements or questions that predominate we can build a 'game plan' to satisfy the other person's key needs at each stage of the thinking process".[2]

Contrast this approach with the traditional selling process, which totally ignores what the client is thinking in favour of following a prescribed set of steps culminating in "the close". Most traditional selling processes run according to the following formula: motivate the person to talk to you, find out their needs, propose solutions, address concerns and finally close.

I find the cognitive map approach particularly appealing because it tests the integrity of the communication at all times. While I can force you to buy by using aggressive closing techniques, I can only *influence* you to buy if I have been able to facilitate your mind's journey in arriving at that decision. The traditional process focuses on achieving the sale. The cognitive map focuses on addressing various logical and emotional needs and then allowing the client to decide to buy.

Let's take a close look at how people make buying decisions and map out the five[*] stages your clients mind will take from their initial feeling of curiosity, resistance or even suspicion to choosing to engage your services as their financial advisor.

Stage 1: Ego

"I am important and want to be treated with respect."

A sales situation immediately creates an emotional polarity. Lambert calls this a "power differential".[3] One party is trying to convince the other party to buy something. Almost every prospective client you start a conversation with will adopt a defensive mental stance. Our subconscious yells "someone is trying to make you think in a way that may not be in your best interests". You can just picture a couple bickering as they travel to their meeting with a financial advisor: "We're just going to find out what it's all about, we're not going to sign up for anything. Let me do the talking. Don't commit to anything."

Contrast this with the assumption that traditional selling makes when it assumes that the client wants to do business with us as long as we can match their needs with our solutions.

Our game plan here is to build rapport with the client. It is crucial to communicate that the purpose of the discussion is to talk about the client's goals and

---

[*] Lambert describes six. I have synthesised these to five which I believe work best for the typical advice conversation.

objectives. Too many professionals feel an urge to speak about what can be delivered, rather than giving a client the courtesy of hearing what they (the client) actually want.

You'll find some real gems on the topics of trust and rapport in the next chapter. But for now, let's stick with the stages of our cognitive map.

Only once the client feels they are being taken seriously by someone they feel comfortable with will their mind progress to the next stage.

Stage 2: I'm okay

*"I already have a point of view and I want it
taken into account."*

Again, traditional selling makes the assumption that our proposed solution is better than our client's current solution. This suggests to the client that they have been embracing a second-rate position and that they've even made a mistake by adopting their current solution. Your prospective client has made a decision (for better or for worse) and will seek to defend it. Most of us react badly when we are told we are wrong.

Our game plan here is to communicate that things have changed. We must be absolutely neutral and make it clear that the changes have nothing to do with, or have been caused by, either ourselves or the client. But we must make it clear that these changes (over which neither of us has any control) have affected the client's ability to achieve their objectives.

Only once our client feels that their current solution may no longer be the most appropriate will they move to their next thought.

Stage 3: Can you help me?

"Will your ideas help me and give me what I want?"

At this point your prospective client is unsettled, but not necessarily in a buying mood. They may have recognised that they do have an issue but aren't convinced that it's worth the effort to address, or whether you are the person from whom they should be seeking a solution. They are thinking about whether to procrastinate and to find a way of simply saying no, or to listen further. If they do bail at this point it's because you have been unable to generate sufficient emotional momentum at Stage 2. Fear not – we'll address this capability over several chapters in this book.

By the time our client's mind reaches Stage 3 you will have some idea why they've put in the effort to meet with you and what they hope to accomplish working with a financial advisor. They're looking for reasons to continue the conversation. Their mind – often subconsciously – is seeking answers to questions like, "Are you the right person to be dealing with? Do I feel that you have the experience and knowledge required to help me? Why should I allow you to assist me?"

Here's your opportunity to describe in very broad brushstrokes how, what you do will enable them to seize the opportunities available to them or to address or avoid the dangers that await them on their current course. You'll also briefly cover your track record and experience with similar clients facing similar issues.

There are two important points to emphasise for this stage:

- At Stage 3 the buyer "owns" their problem (or wants to convert an opportunity). Don't make the mistake of trying to resell this to them. Their mind is trying to determine whether it's worth the effort to solve the problem and is seeking the comfort of knowing (feeling) that you are the right person to work with because you possess both the expertise and a track record of delivering on that expertise.

- I've deliberately used the words "broad brushstrokes" and "briefly" to describe the way you manage the conversation when you believe your client's mind rests in Stage 3. Please understand that, at this stage, your client has not chosen to work with you. They are looking for reasons to. If they sense that you have made that assumption – and they most assuredly will if you start launching into any detail – they will emotionally retreat. The assumptive close is one of the most aggressive tactics of old-school selling and I feel that it is particularly inappropriate for a professional to use.

Your tactics in Stage 3 are not dissimilar to those used by a champion snooker player. Your objective is to set up the next play. To create a vacuum for your client to move into. Your conversation could almost be summarised as follows:

"You've got a problem. We both agree on that. I've got both the expertise and track record for solving such problems. I've done it before. Here are some (very high level) ideas. I know what I'm doing. I can deliver. And I've got many satisfied clients who would agree with me. [Pause] So where should we go from here?"

Stage 4: Tell me more

"What is your idea?"

Your client is now hungry for information.

Stage 4 is the tipping point. Your client is now looking for reasons to do business with you. They are engaged. They are curious. They want facts, information, any insight that they believe will equip them to make a good decision.

You need to cover a lot of ground here – this is the only time that you should do the bulk of the talking. Jump up and use your whiteboard. Describe some of the strategies you're likely to employ. Model scenarios on your fancy software. Explain the process you take your clients through – both initially and the post-sale care and support you'll provide. By logically linking your activity with your client's objectives you fuse the two and thus position yourself as part and parcel of the desired solution.

Emotion will make the sale, but logic will grease the wheels.

Use logic carefully to build resolve and confidence in your client:

- Logic removes any lingering doubts (can this be done?) and is appreciated by your client (I'm not being treated like the village idiot).
- Logic provides your client with the support that they may need to sell the idea to themselves and others. It protects their ego by equipping them with an ability to defend their position when challenged by others: "You should be careful working with a financial advisor. Haven't you read in the papers that they're only in it for the commission?"
- Logic supports the client's perception that you really understand their needs and made suggestions that appear to provide appropriate solutions.

We need to counter the mental objection "can this be done?" by describing how we will implement our advice. We don't want the client thinking "I like what I'm hearing, but I can't see how to make it all happen."

As with all communication, it is not only about what we say, but how we say it. We need to remain in rapport with our client while providing all this information.

Stage 5: The close

"Am I being pressured?"

You have now presented your case for securing your prospective client's business. But you can still blow the sale if you have a lapse in taste and resort to a clumsy closing technique.

Once you have communicated all the information you believe relevant and have responded to all your client's questions, simply summarise the key facts and ask for agreement to proceed. Then keep quiet. Silence exerts its own pressure.

If you have succeeded at moving your client along each step of the process, they will simply feel comfortable to do business with you and ask a question along the lines of "so where do we go from here?"

Again, cognitive mapping and traditional selling differ at this point. Traditional selling relies on a range of closes. Professionals feel particularly uncomfortable using a close because its purpose is so obvious. It suggests to the client that they are now being corralled into saying "yes".

Cognitive mapping explains that clients are wary of being coerced into making a decision. They don't want to feel pressured and every traditional selling close is designed to apply pressure. Our game plan here is to simply remain silent and wait for our client to make up their mind.

If the client raises an objection, we deal with the specific objection. We do not restate our case. After providing a response, we again remain silent and allow the client to lead.

In Chapter 4, *The power of questions*, I'll provide you with a few questions that will enable you to comfortably set up your close and provide your client with the respect and courtesy to make up their own mind on whether they choose to proceed. Chapter 8 will take you through the close step by step.

Linking the cognitive map to enabling capabilities

As foreshadowed in the *Introduction*, your ability to commercialise your specialist knowledge, skills and expertise rests totally on how successful you are at converting curious prospects into committed clients. This ability is wholly dependent on the quality of your enabling skills.

The table below shows which enabling skills are required to successfully progress a client's mind to the point where they commit to doing business with you:

What your client is thinking	Capabilities required to progress this thinking
Stage 1: Ego • Am I being shown respect? • Is this person trying to take advantage of me? Trying to get me to do something that is not in my best interest?	• Ability to communicate that you can be trusted (covered in Chapter 2) • Ability to build rapport (covered in Chapter 2) • Listening skills (covered in Chapter 2) • Ability to frame the meeting via the use of an Agenda Statement or a Statement of Intent (covered in Chapter 3) • Questioning skills (covered in Chapter 4)

What your client is thinking	Capabilities required to progress this thinking
Stage 2: I'm okay • I already have a point of view • I understand what's good for me • I have a solution in place that I feel the need to defend • I've got this far on my own without your help	• Questioning skills (covered in Chapter 4) • Persuasive skills (covered in Chapter 5) • Storytelling skills (covered in Chapter 6)
Stage 3: Can you help me? • You've unsettled me a bit • Is this worth the effort? • Why should I allow you to assist me? • Are you the right person to be dealing with? • Do I feel that you have the required knowledge and experience?	• Ability to build rapport (covered in Chapter 2) • Persuasive skills (covered in Chapter 5) • Ability to communicate the value you will bring to the relationship in a way that it is perceived as being of value by your client (covered in Chapter 7)
Stage 4: Tell me more • I recognise that I have a need and want to understand how you can help me • Do I like what I'm hearing? • Am I feeling comfortable with the proposed solution? • Do I think that what I'm being told can actually be done?	• Persuasive skills (covered in Chapter 5) • Ability to communicate high-level processes and solutions using media such as whiteboard, notepad and planning software. Liberal use of visual support such as diagrams and graphs. Limited use of technical jargon. (Predominantly technical capabilities and thus not addressed in this book)

What your client is thinking	Capabilities required to progress this thinking
Stage 5: The close • Am I being pressured? • Is my right to decide being respected?	• Ability to frame the meeting via the use of an Agenda Statement or a Statement of Intent (covered in Chapter 3) • Ability to close with a summary, question and silence (covered in Chapter 8)

The cognitive map is not necessarily linear. Nor does it have to start at Stage 1 …

At this point you may feel that my description of the cognitive map is too neat, too linear. And you would be right. By describing the map in a five-stage sequence I could leave you with the impression that this is a bit of a tick-the-box journey:

• Satisfy the client that you are worthy of trust and that they can feel comfortable with you.

• Create some discomfort by discussing how their current solution does not stack up any longer.

• And so on …

The key takeaways here are to appreciate that the map explains both the mental journey your client needs to travel before choosing to work with you and where they are on that journey. After mastering the contents of this book – and especially this chapter – you'll be able to spot your client's mental state and adjust your approach and conversation to provide the necessary input. As

Lambert puts it: "to satisfy the other person's key needs at each stage of the thinking process".[4]

Reading your client's mind in practice

You'll find spotting where your clients are becomes easier and easier. Here a few examples of common client comments and the stage where their mind is currently resting:

- "I feel I'm just not getting the kind of support and service I should be getting from the advisor who is looking after me" **Stage 3**
- "My banker/accountant suggested I speak with you. I haven't really worked with a financial advisor before" **Stage 1**
- "I'm not sure if you can help me. I'm not married, don't have any kids and don't really need insurance" **Stage 2**
- "My mate's getting much better returns with his investments than my guy is doing for me" **Stage 3**
- "I think that the fee you've quoted sounds very dear" **Stage 3**
- "You mentioned something about stepped premiums and level premiums. Can you just explain again what these mean?" **Stage 4**

Your challenge is to ensure that the conversation you're having with your client aligns with what they need from that conversation at that moment. As soon as you detect that you've lost this alignment – and you'll only know this by listening carefully to what your client is saying or asking – assess at which stage your client's mind is operating and bring the conversation to that point.

Your ability to be able to spot the stage is crucial because the journey may not be linear. It seldom is. Let me expand on this point using the follow scenario:

Sitting in front of you is a retired couple who have been referred to you by some friends who are your clients. The conversation is taking place in Stage 3 and you are responding to their "can you help me" need. You're on song and happily describing how many of your current clients face the same worries and issues that they (the couple sitting in front of you) are currently wrestling with. You get a bit carried away and mention a few names and even provide a brief example of how you've helped them. Suddenly you detect a mood change. The couple look at each other and one says, "We're very private people. We really don't want any of our friends to know about our financial position." It's that easy to skip from Stage 3 to Stage 1. Your apparent casual approach to speaking about other clients has negatively impacted the retired couple's perception of your trustworthiness. You will never get to Stage 5 unless you move the conversation back to Stage 1 and repair the damage. If you are successful in achieving this, you'll find that your clients will bypass Stage 2 and continue to seek the input they need in Stage 3.

Not only can your client's mind flick backwards and forwards between steps, but in some cases they may skip a step altogether. This typically happens where a client is referred by someone they have deep trust in. The conversation can flow like this:

"My accountant speaks very highly of you. She says you are an absolute professional and thoroughly discreet. I've worked with my accountant for 20 years and if she says you're the best person to work with, then that's good enough for me. I know that she's briefed you on the issues I'm having with the investments in my self-managed super. What ideas have you got to improve my position?" Straight to Stage 4 from the start.

A very similar conversation, but with a different stage from which to start…

"My accountant speaks very highly of you. He says you are an absolute professional and thoroughly discreet. I've worked with my accountant for 20 years and he says you're the best person to work with. I know that he's briefed you on the issues I'm having with the investments in my self-managed super. Could you give me some idea how you help people in my position?" Here the conversation kicks off in Stage 3.

How the cognitive map answers the "four questions"

In their book *Power Questions*, Andrew Sobel and Jerold Panas describe four hurdle questions in their chapter When the Sale is Stuck.[5] Sobel and Panas explain that, before any sale can take place, each of these questions has to be answered in the affirmative. Paraphrased to be particularly relevant for the sale of financial advice, the questions are:

1. Does your client have a problem?
2. Do they own the problem?
3. Do they really want to fix the problem?
4. Do they think that you're the right person to work with?

What fascinated me was the obvious link between buyer psychology as described in the cognitive map and these hurdle questions.

The first two questions go to the heart of Stage 2. If you are not able to help your client understand that they have a problem, and that this problem can have unpleasant consequences, then there is very little chance that they will progress to Stage 3. Why should they be at all interested in how you can help them if they don't believe they need any help?

Questions 3 and 4 are what Stage 3 is all about. Will you be able to motivate them sufficiently to address their problem and have you presented yourself in a sufficiently compelling way so that they believe that you have the answers?

The cognitive map and Sinek's *why*

I've been very influenced by a book written by Simon Sinek called *Start with Why*. It's a great read, but if you want to save yourself time you'll get the gist from his presentation on ted.com.

Sinek's thesis is that greatness comes from clarity of purpose, knowing your *why*. He explains that everyone knows *what* they do. These are the day-to-day tasks that occupy their time. Or, from a business perspective, the service or product it provides. Many people understand *how* they perform their roles – the processes involved in delivering the *what*. These businesses focus on execution. They seek to build competitive advantage via leaner processes and less waste. Far fewer people and businesses are clear on *why* they do *what* they do. They lack both purpose and perspective. Sinek explains that most training, most marketing material, most corporate mission statements, most handbooks, and most anything we encounter in our business lives tends to focus on *what*, sometimes *how* but seldom *why*. Using examples, Sinek shows that those rare companies that start with *why*, rather than defining themselves by *what* they do, tower above the rest. He uses arguably the world's most successful company, Apple, to support his case. Apple's *what* is obvious – they make computers and phones. But so do many other companies – Hewlett Packard, Dell, Nokia and Samsung. Why is Apple so unique, such a world-beater? It's because they know their *why*. Apple's *why* is to challenge the status quo. To innovate. To disrupt. Apple attracts rebels. People who like to lift a finger at the establishment. Their products look different. They are elegant, intuitive, sexy. Apple seldom discounts. And when they do it is usually by a miserly 10%. Walk into your local Apple store and you'll see that Apple doesn't have employees – they have a tribe of passionate zealots.

Now overlay Sinek's philosophy with our cognitive map. Most financial advisors introduce *what* they do into the conversation as early as they can. It's ground that they feel comfortable on. But our *what* is akin to Stage 4. We need to get through a few hurdles first. So let's *start with why*. *Why* is the essence of Stages 1 and 2. Why have you chosen to practice as a financial advisor? Why should I trust you? Why should I invest my valuable time listening to you? Why is there a problem with my current position? Why should I feel any urgency to do anything about it? *How* is the essence of Stage 3. How does your process work (so that I can decide whether you're the right person to run with)? How do you propose to solve my problem, help me seize the opportunity (so I can consider whether all this is worth the effort)? Great thinking tends to align, to compliment, to confirm. Just like Sinek's *why* philosophy and Lambert's cognitive map.

Final word

The logic of the cognitive map is wonderfully intuitive. It simply makes sense. I've trained numerous advisors to use this map, coached them in its application and observed the impact it had on their confidence, the quality of their conversations and their ability to convert curious prospects to committed clients.

The ability to motivate someone to take action is a highly prized and rewarded skill. There are many people who have great wisdom and can provide substantial value to others. The challenge is to receive a commercial return for that wisdom, that expertise. This is the preserve of enabling capabilities.

Key points from this chapter

- Cognitive psychology provides us with a map that empowers us to peek into our client's mind and see where they are on the buying journey.
- The map describes the five stages your client's mind will travel through before choosing to do business with you.
- Various enabling capabilities are required for you to successfully progress your client through each stage.
- The journey described in the cognitive map is not linear and your client may both jump stages and move back to earlier stages.
- Skilful use of the cognitive map allows you to understand where your client is on their buying journey and therefore direct your conversation to provide the input needed at that stage.

Chapter 2:

Lowering the defences – how to build trust and rapport

"The role of trust in business relationships is a greater determinant of success than anything else."

Charles H. Green
The Trusted Advisor

With just a few months before year-end exams, all the major accounting firms descended onto the campus of my alma mater, the University of the Witwatersrand, more commonly referred to as "Wits". Their mission was to identify and recruit whatever talent existed in the graduating year. Among us students there was definitely an order of preference. First prize was a blue chip firm that had both a local and international presence. This would ensure our marketability around the world and provide us with a brand that opened doors. The bluest of the blue chips was Arthur Andersen & Co., the only genuine world-wide partnership with a Swiss-based ownership structure and a world-wide fee sharing arrangement (particularly lucrative for South African based partners due to the ever-depreciating local currency). The other firms were international brands, but with local ownership, similar to a franchise arrangement.

To my delight I was offered a contract to commence my articles with the mighty AA & Co. Within a few weeks of graduating, the firm flew all of its first-year clerks to a small town in the southern Netherlands called Veldhoven where we would undergo an intensive two-week induction course. The facilities were spectacular, the quality of the training superb, the engagement level of the recruits right out of an Anthony Robbins book. The twenty-odd South Africans were joined by about two hundred other recruits from the UK, India and several other countries (Arthur Andersen had a similar facility at St Charles, Illinois, hence the absence of any Americans on our program). Each of us learnt exactly the same process, the same methods to record the results of our audit procedures and were (willingly) indoctrinated with the history of the firm, its culture, its values and its competitive advantages. The message was compelling – because we used the same methodology and the same language, we were best positioned to service the global giants, the biggest of the fee payers.

Fast forward seven years. My accounting articles are well behind me. I was lazing on a bed in a resort on Australia's Sunshine Coast half watching TV, half watching my little daughters playing with fuzzy felt. Suddenly my attention was totally on the TV where Joe Beradino, the senior international partner of Arthur Andersen, was in serious damage control. Seems like the firm's Houston office had happily signed off the financial statements of a company called Enron, which had just filed for bankruptcy.

The spectacular rise and equally impressive fall of Enron has been well-documented in movies and books. The trial of their top two executives – Kenneth Lay and Jeffrey Skilling – made compelling TV viewing for years. What happened at Arthur Andersen took a lower profile. Rumours started circulating of professional negligence. Things got worse when there was talk of auditing files being destroyed. A cheeky mate of mine sent me a video attached to an email. The short video showed residents of a ground floor apartment remarking with surprise that it was snowing in summer. The video panned up along the front of the building. On the top level – in offices bearing the name Arthur Andersen – we saw people furiously shredding documents and throwing the confetti out of the window giving the appearance of snow to those living below. Soon after Beradino's "it's business as usual folks, nothing to see here, move along" TV appearance, major clients began moving to other firms along with many of the more marketable partners. The phones rang hot, "if I can retain my partnership at your firm, I'll bring along most of my clients". Just a year or so later, the world's biggest professional services firm, employing around 85,000 people, ceased to exist.

Arthur Andersen destroyed its credibility. It was no longer trustworthy. Therefore it couldn't continue to operate. Financial services are a complex, intangible, often opaque business. Where a provider cannot be trusted – whether a giant multinational or a sole practitioner – there is no business to be done.

What is trust?

If you Google the meaning of trust you'll find some pretty common definitions. Here's a typical example:

"A firm belief in the reliability, truth, or ability of someone or something."

The key word here is "belief". Trust is perceived. I've done many workshops and talks on this topic and it seems that I always upset someone by suggesting that it is not so much whether a person is an honest straight-shooter with high moral values and a clean skin who always plays by the rules. Most people see themselves as honest. It is whether the person sitting in front of them believes this or not. And if that's what's important, what can you do to make this happen?

Some professions seem to have more inherent trust than others. The trustworthiness of medical specialists is hardly ever questioned. Apart from perhaps seeking a second opinion, we are quite happy to literally place our lives in the hands of someone we hardly know. Anything they tell us is gospel.

We tend to give the benefit of the doubt to lawyers and accountants. They are old, established professions. We understand that these practitioners have cleared fairly high hurdles and believe their professions to be well regulated. We accept what they tell us.

Not for the financial advisor. When it comes to being perceived as trustworthy, we face headwinds. The origins of these headwinds lie partly in our past conduct (and, in some cases, current) and partly due to the ignorance – or perhaps naivety – of the people we work with. Whatever the cause, the consequence is our profession lacks the necessary inherent trust and therefore we need to build it at the start almost each and every time we meet with a new prospective client.

I say "almost" because, as I explained in the previous chapter, trust can be transferred where we meet a prospective client who has been referred by someone who they trust and who trusts us. You believe your boss is a smart and astute person. You have complete faith in her judgement. You mention that you're somewhat concerned with the lack of attention you have given the investment in your superannuation fund. Your boss tells you that she works with a very knowledgeable, experienced and discrete advisor and asks whether you would like an introduction. "I'd really appreciate that", you say. A week later you're sitting in front of that advisor. What's going through your mind? Are you worried about being respected? About being taken advantage of? Of course not. Someone you trust has just facilitated a meeting with someone they trust. The trust is transferred.

I'll try not to sound too cynical but it seems to me that trust is in short supply. There are very few deep-trust relationships like the one I've described above. Thanks to the conflict of interests associated with advisors' fees linked to products sold, thanks to the near hysteria of some journalists who see financial advice as an unnecessary cost that slowly depletes desperately-needed retirement savings, thanks to the politicians who see an opportunity to curry favour with a vulnerable electorate, thanks to product failure, financial market volatility and a host of other factors, the people who seek our advice usually arrive at our offices with a wary and defensive mindset. If we fail to build sufficient trust we have no hope of moving past Stage 1. This chapter will provide you with an understanding of what trust is and how you can consistently present yourself as trustworthy: someone worthy of being trusted.

How to maximise your trustworthiness

In their superb book on the topic of trust, *The Trusted Advisor*, David Maister, Charles Green and Robert Galford provide us with a model that defines the components of trust. Understanding this model will equip you to appreciate how what you say, how you present yourself and even how your business is set up can either enhance or harm your trustworthiness.

Their model looks like this:

$$T = \frac{C + R + I}{S}$$

Now don't panic if maths isn't your forte. There are no numbers involved. Let me run through the variables while you take the opportunity to reflect on how you stack up with each.

Trustworthiness

T is your overall trustworthiness. This can be improved by developing the skills, mindset and business model that affect the other four variables.

Credibility

C is how credible your client perceives you to be. Prior to becoming a fan of Maister & Co.'s formula, I believed that credibility was the all-important ingredient that enabled an advisor to make successful progress past Stage 1. I'm fond of quoting Professor Jay Conger, who wrote in the *Harvard Business Review* "Credibility is the cornerstone of effective persuasion. Without it the persuader won't be given the time of day".[6] But I now clearly realise that being credible is not the same as being trusted. It's simply an important part.

The word credibility is derived from the Latin word "credibilis" which means "to believe". I know this both from a Google search and from being an unwilling and extremely disengaged member of my school's Latin class for five years. There is much more to being trustworthy than simply telling the truth and sticking to facts.

You have quite a few ways to maximise your credibility in the eyes of another. Let me walk you through some of these.

Education, expertise and experience

Your qualifications and your tenure have a strong impact on perceived credibility. People will regard you as more credible not just because of what you know, but for *how long* you've actually demonstrated that knowledge. The two need to work in tandem.

Regarding education, suffice to say that the relevance of your qualifications, your areas of specialisation and the institution you studied through all play a part. I've seen firsthand the ease with which advisors with Masters, and in a couple of cases with Doctorates, established their credibility with their clients. As our market continues to mature, and as our clients become more aware that the value of the advice relationship is to be found in the advisor, not the product, there will be even greater scrutiny around the quality of our formal education.

Experience plays a critical part too. Picture the scene. You're a keen runner and your enthusiasm has led to wear and tear on your knee. It really gets sore after a few kilometres and, after a short consultation with your GP, you're referred to an orthopaedic surgeon. I said earlier that medical specialists are the most credible of all. They speak the gospel. After an initial consultation and a trip to get some X-rays, you're back in the surgeon's consulting room. Your worst fears are realised when the surgeon informs you that you require a full knee reconstruction. You're digesting this bad news when you think to ask what kind of success rate the surgeon has experienced with knee op clients to date. Your surgeon replies, "Actually, I've only worked on knees for the last month or two, my speciality is elbows and hands."

This may be a somewhat constructed story, but the point is clear. Without experience, and some track record of successfully delivering on the solutions your clients seek, you will not have maximum credibility. I'm told by several advisors that when they discuss actual insurance claims made by their clients (or beneficiaries of clients) they can feel the impact this has on credibility and ultimately trust. Don't panic if you are new to the profession of financial advice, you can compensate by having a strong hand in the other components of credibility.

Media, awards, recognition, white papers and websites

Your credibility is boosted when you are recognised as being credible by others. Appearing in the media, receiving awards in the field of financial advice and being recognised for some advice-related achievement are credibility boosters. Writing articles that are then published in an industry journal is a credibility booster. Publish a book? Even better. So is a well-presented website.

Brigid Asquith-Hunt, who does excellent work delivering advisor capability, provides us with a powerful credibility-boosting strategy. She suggests advisors write a White Paper. This is more than just an article because it requires research, helps you understand your market better and increases your credibility in that market. Your first step is to identify a niche market in which you'd like to raise your profile and credibility. Step two is to interview centres of influence in that market – heads of associations, leading practitioners, people who provide supporting services and any others who can provide relevant insights into the financial needs and opportunities that are common to that niche. You'll not only collect excellent market intelligence but, more importantly, you'll create a network of influential people who recognise the effort you are putting in to understand their situation. Step three requires that you document your findings in a White Paper. You would review the status quo and highlight issues, needs, opportunities, and possible solutions. Your final step is to distribute your Paper. You can do this through industry publications that service your niche market, by asking associations to distribute your findings to their members and directly to selected prospective clients. Several factors impact and enhance your credibility: the expertise you gain through this exercise, the centres of influence you create and via the publication of your material. You may even be asked to present your work at conferences and professional development days.

Dress, offices…

I don't wear a tie and I'm not the world's nattiest dresser. But I appreciate the impact that a well-fitted Italian suit, tailored and monogrammed shirt and beautifully-made silk tie can have. My friend Brad is the ultimate power dresser. All of the above and more. I bumped into him at a busy Sydney intersection. We chatted for a few moments while the group I was with walked ahead. When I caught up with my colleagues they were curious as to what he did. "Is he an investment banker?" one of them asked.

Some people pay a fortune for fancy offices with the right address. They're making a call that the extra rent paid is more than returned with the additional business they'll receive through this credibility kicker.

On the flip side, being pound foolish can tarnish your credibility. I had a very brief coaching engagement with an advisor who operated out of a home office. On arriving I rang the intercom and was instructed to make my way down a passage that ran along the side of the house. I'd find the office at the end of this. The lock clicked and I walked through the front gate. Melbourne was in the midst of a multi-year drought and this showed in the barren and unkempt front yard. I walked across to the narrow passageway and startled a little dog who started barking at me. I hurried towards the dusty glass sliding door and entered the office. My client greeted me by firstly apologising for all the barking and then reflecting that he should have warned me to watch where I was walking because he hadn't had time to clean up after the dog.

Credibility is also influenced by body language, eye contact and the amount of preparation done before the meeting. There are lots of great books on these topics if you have an urge to drill deeper.

Words and respect

The words you use and the respect you show others have an impact. Your credibility will be influenced by any bias, disrespect, prejudice or any suggestion of non-compliance in your words. I've picked this up and challenged advisors many times. I've experienced chauvinism ("I'll get my girl to make us some copies"), a lack of respect for staff and colleagues ("he's not the sharpest pencil in the box"), or suggesting that a client provide unreliable or incomplete answers to a questionnaire ("don't worry about all your visits to the doctor, just record the last few").

Credibility is enhanced by admitting that you don't know

Admitting that you don't know the answer to a client's question will boost your credibility in their eyes. By showing weakness, showing that you are vulnerable, you communicate that you are happy to expose yourself, warts and all. The person in front of you thinks – either consciously or subconsciously – "hey, if this advisor is prepared to admit that he doesn't know something, I can be more confident that what he does tell me is probably true".

Nick Murray is an internationally-recognised author and commentator on the subject of financial advice and the professionals who deliver this service. We'll hear much more from him in Chapter 7. He, too, supports the notion that we need to be absolutely candid about what we know and what we don't when he states, "The earliest and strongest impression you want to convey to prospective clients is one of trustworthiness, much more than of competence".[7]

Reliability

R is how reliable your client perceives you to be. Your credibility is inherent – it exists thanks to your qualifications, your track record, your office, your suit. Unlike credibility, reliability cannot be inherent, it must be demonstrated. Reliability should be the easiest variable in the trust model to score high on as it's really about discipline, good habits and good processes.

Reliability can be demonstrated by being punctual. By setting expectations with clients and following through. Say you receive an enquiry from a prospective client. Set the expectation by committing to a time frame, "I'll have my Introduction Pack emailed to you before noon." Then make absolutely sure you do just that. It's a small thing to do, but it already plants the seed in your client's mind: this person does what they say, this person follows through, I can *rely* on this person.

Reliability is often dependent on your business's processes and systems. Even a small advisory business is characterised by lots of activity. Reliability needs a good task management system that directs activity along well thought through processes. Most current financial advisor software has this capability. "To do" notes jotted on the proverbial back of the envelope or the nearest scrap of paper will ensure dropped balls, label you in the eyes of the affected party as unreliable and, in that way, damage your trustworthiness.

Reliability is also influenced by the culture of your business. There's a great book by Ken Blanchard in his *One Minute Manager* series called *The One Minute Manager Meets the Monkey*. A monkey is simply the next move. Blanchard asks "who in your firm is responsible for the next move?" Do you and the people you rely on "own" each task? I spent a very frustrating six months working at a small dealer group where the CEO was always vague about who was responsible for various action items. He'd say things like "we must really start working on a new corporate brochure" or, "we're receiving a lot of enquiries from advisors interested in joining our group that need to be followed up". This drove me up the wall and I soon insisted that each suggestion be reformulated into an action item and recorded in formal minutes. He agreed to this but floored me at the next meeting by asking that the minutes from the previous meeting (which contained completed, half completed and completely ignored action items) be accepted and then went straight on to the new agenda. Blanchard remarks in the book that he often walks into an office and sees monkeys sitting on the filing cabinet, hanging from the lights, snoozing in half-opened drawers. This is just a metaphor for the number of tasks, commitments and promises that fall through the cracks in so many firms.

To be perceived as reliable you require discipline, culture, processes and systems so that a dropped ball is a rare occurrence.

Intimacy

I stands for intimacy, which is really about your ability to build rapport and to make your clients feel at ease in your presence. Many established financial advisors tend to rate themselves quite highly in this area. This is probably because the opportunity to talk with lots of people about their financial wellbeing attracted extroverts and practitioners who considered themselves to be a "people's person". That certainly was the case when Shultz's waiters handed out sizzling sausages and I stood waiting nervously to play "Scotland the Brave" on my bagpipes. With the shift in financial advice from product to service, and as our market becomes more sophisticated and discerning, and as the acceptance of the need for financial advice becomes mainstream, the profession has attracted – and continues to attract – more and more people who are less salespeople and more technical specialists. It takes the technical specialist a few months to realise that, when it comes to financial advice, being an expert is not enough to be successful. That the value of technical skills can only be unlocked with enabling skills. That the ability to build trust and to be perceived as trustworthy is an important enabling skill and, in turn, the ability to build rapport is as important now as it was in the days of Shultz.

Like all enabling skills, the ability to build rapport – to connect with people, to make people feel comfortable in your presence – can be learnt and practised. There are numerous books on this topic and countless ideas that authors share. I've found the thinking of Dale Carnegie and Daniel Goleman particularly relevant to the early part of advisor-client conversations where the necessity to build rapport is absolutely vital.

Listening

There are some gems in Dale Carnegie's great work, *How to Win Friends and Influence People*. The one that has always stuck with me is his comment about listening: "Listening is one of the highest compliments we can pay anyone".[8] This observation was captured in a very effective bank advertising campaign many years later. One of Australia's Big Four – Westpac – ran a series of TV adverts promoting their financial advice services. They didn't depict a glorious retirement. They didn't suggest that somehow their funds would perform a bit better than their competitors. No. They promised to listen. In each scenario we saw clients intent on communicating their issues. Westpac used people we could identify with – the two business partners, one expressive and emotive, the other quiet and patient. There was a clichéd married couple with a dominating wife and nerdish husband. Like normal people, they explained their situation in a self-absorbed way (it's about me), their thinking confused, inarticulate; their conversation moving all over the place. And while they got all this angst off their chests, the Westpac advisor remained silent. He listened. At one point he looked like he was going to interrupt to clarify something, but as the client continued to talk he caught himself, remained silent and continued to listen. What a powerful message! Kudos to whoever put those adverts together.

People will love you for listening to them because hardly anyone does this. Not in the times of Dale Carnegie, and certainly not now. We are all so keen to get our point of view across, so keen to make ourselves heard.

My late dad was the king of commandeering the dinner table conversation. He was exceptionally well-read and had a strong opinion on most things. His greatest joy was sharing his insights with those around him. (As an aside, I have most definitely inherited this quality from him and require enormous patience from those dear to me when I get going.) I once remember my dad remarking how much he enjoyed the previous night's event and how friendly and engaging he found the people seated near him. To this my mother replied, "Yes, Shlomo, that's because you never gave them a chance to speak." It worked on him. It worked for Westpac. And it will work for you.

There's more power for those who choose to remain silent, or at least where you choose to let your client do the majority of the talking. Not only will you build rapport and intimacy, you will impact your client's confidence in another important way. A person who has been allowed to fully communicate their point of view trusts the listener more because they believe you have understood their position. While this involves credibility more than intimacy, credibility is enhanced because of intimacy, the combination resulting in a significant boost to trustworthiness. Let me explain. Your credibility is enhanced by what you know, how much of an expert in the field of financial advice you are perceived to be. But your client's thinking does not stop at just what you know about advice; it continues to ask itself about what you know about their particular circumstances. When a client decides that you not only know what you are talking about in a general sense, but are able to apply that knowledge and expertise to their specific circumstances, their trust and faith in you magnifies. The former is gained through training and experience, the latter through listening.

Finding common ground

A prospective client is a stranger. Even if referred. The easiest way to reduce the inevitable tension that this involves is to find common ground. Where does your life and that of the person sitting in front of you overlap? Do you have similar family circumstances? Any common hobbies or interests? Share an interest in the same sport, TV program, travel destination? Did you grow up in the same town? Did your schools play sport against each other? Bottom line here is that people feel more comfortable (read intimate) with people with whom they share something in common.

As a guy with a thick Johannesburg accent, it's easy for me to connect and feel comfortable with most South African immigrants. When my kids started school it was easy to connect with the parents of their new mates. Many of these parents are now close friends. Good common ground can even be very specific. I was observing an advisor during a first meeting with a prospective client. One of the areas I was looking out for was his ability to build rapport through searching out common ground. He asked about the client's family and, after a few minutes, discovered that one of her children suffered from Celiac disease, a condition where the body is very sensitive to foods with gluten. The advisor's son had the same condition and in no time they were comparing notes and speaking like old acquaintances.

The "old school tie", the bond that exists between all those who have served their country, the passion that unites people who support the same sports team, singer, band, movement, cause, are all examples of the emotional glue that awaits the advisor who is thoughtful and proactive about discovering what common ground they share with those who've entered their office for the first time.

Emotional intelligence

Credibility is inherent, reliability demonstrated and intimacy sensed. You can listen and you can deliberately discover common ground, but how do you know whether you have created rapport? This vibe, this feeling is the preserve of emotional intelligence. Daniel Goleman is the pop star here. In his book *Emotional Intelligence*, he shone the spotlight on what was a previously obscure area of psychology. The definition of emotional intelligence can be summed up as an "ability to identify and manage your own emotions and the emotions of others".[9]

A lack of empathy, or ability to detect the vibe, is a hindrance for a financial advisor. There is so much communication that takes place outside of the spoken word. Advisors without empathy struggle to create intimacy and thus fail to maximise their trustworthiness. If you believe that you may be weak in this area, consider investing time in understanding the basics of emotional intelligence and then working with a coach to implement these.

Communication competency

I'm starting to move into the complex here and that's not the purpose of this book. But I'd be doing you a disservice if I didn't acknowledge this topic, even in just a fleeting manner.

In our search for common ground we explore where our life's journeys have overlapped. Our intention is to create intimacy by getting the person in front of us to think to themselves something like, "Hey! This advisor is just like me. We both (insert what you've discovered that you both feel some passion about)."

We can be a lot more sophisticated in our search for common ground. And here is where Neuro-Linguistic Programming (NLP) can support our efforts. Let me make full disclosure that I'm an absolute journeyman on this topic. I have not invested anywhere near the time required to master its concepts … but I have discovered some very useful insights.

What NLP has taught me is that we are very different in how we relate to the outside world. Bluntly put, I now appreciate that there is no such thing as "reality". What each of us believes to be reality is more a product of how the structures and filters of our mind interpret the input from our five senses. NLP suggests, and I'm happy to

41

buy this, that by developing an ability to understand how we process input, we can start to appreciate different ways of interpreting the same input and thereby better understanding and empathise with how others interpret life.

So how could this be useful to you to develop intimacy with your clients?

NLP recognises that we each have a preferred learning style – visual, auditory or kinesthetic. Some of us learn best by seeing, others by hearing and a smaller percentage by physically doing. I'm a strong visual. I read, I take notes. My friend Tama is auditory. He loves listening to lectures and learning while he drives. I know that my concentration span when listening is very poor. My mind wanders and I'm easily distracted.

Spotting a particular learning style among your clients is not easy (or at least, I tend to struggle). So mix up your communication styles. Talk to them, draw diagrams on a notepad. Jump up and use the whiteboard.

An understanding of some meta programs is also useful. Meta programs are the ways we process input – those filters I mentioned earlier. By aligning the way we provide input with our client's preferred way of processing that input, we give ourselves the very best chance of getting our client to think, "Hey, this advisor is just like me. Not sure what it is. I just feel very comfortable with his style … the way he speaks to me … I feel that this is someone I can trust."

Here are a few examples of meta programs that are particularly relevant to the client-advisor experience:

Detail vs. Brevity – You will annoy a client who wants to cut to the bottom line if you are a thorough, long-winded, pedantic, detail-oriented person. And vice versa. If you sense that your client is mentally snapping their fingers, get a move on. If your client makes it easier for you by asking for a high level snapshot, jettison your preferred style and align with theirs.

Formal vs. Relaxed – You can alienate your client if your natural tendency is to talk like an academic and they are hip, cool and informal. And vice versa. I'm not suggesting that you sound like you've just stepped off campus, but I'm sure you can imagine how a conversation goes where one person is using stiff, multi-syllable words embedded in long, grammatically-correct sentences while the other is using slang and loose sentence structure. It's oil and water, and a recipe for discomfort.

Excitement vs. Risk Averse – This has nothing to do with investment risk and everything to do with how we see the world. If we're talking to our new client about travel to unusual places (my ex-boss Richard told me about his flight to the Galapagos Islands in a beat-up, single-propeller plane), camping in the wilds, or about a heavy night on the town with the boys and they are conservative, risk-averse types, realise that you have introduced some discomfort into the relationship. Some people live very full lives; others prefer a more moderate experience. As my friend Alan often says, "I'm always happy to sleep under the stars. Five stars." Be aware of where your client stands.

43

High Energy vs. Reserved – I'm a high-energy person. I speak fast and fairly loudly. I gesticulate a lot and you'll often hear passion and urgency in my tone. This can grate people who simply prefer a bit less intensity. I particularly noticed this in a colleague of mine, Allan. He's a lovely man. Quiet, gentle, warm, measured. When I sat next to him at all-day Leadership Team meetings, I sensed how much my natural behaviour put him on edge and made a big effort to pull myself in.

There is much, much more to be written on meta programs. If what I've written sparks an interest, jump onto the internet to find out more. However, I'm not sure that you'll get a big return by developing expert capability here. I believe that by being aware that people seek some familiarity, some common ground in those they meet for the first time, should suffice at this point. Be alert to those who are very different from you. Appreciate that finding common ground is useful and constructive for intimacy to develop. If need be, rein in your most obvious differences and focus on those parts of the trust formula where you believe you will obtain more leverage.

Confidentiality

Intimacy is strongly influenced by you being able to communicate that you can maintain the confidence of others. Even best friends and family tend to keep their financial affairs secret. Do not be tempted to make reference to any of your clients other than in an anonymous reference. Testimonials only give you permission to discuss what's disclosed in them. When asked anything specific about any client, your answer should be along the lines of, "I don't discuss any of my clients' affairs. In fact, I don't even discuss who is and who isn't a client of mine. I'm sure that if you choose to do business with me you would appreciate this commitment."

Let's now move to the final variable in the equation – and the one that has given so many financial advisors such grief.

Self-Orientation

S stands for self-orientation, or simply, your priorities. Our profession is emerging from a culture that has been accused of putting sales above service. Of putting our priorities above the needs of our clients. There has never been a type of Hippocratic Oath for the financial advisor.

S is the denominator of our model. It means that the greater our self-orientation, the greater the tendency to place self-interest above that of the client. And this results in us being seen as less trustworthy.

In the 70s financial advisors were called agents and brokers. They were responsible for selling financial products. The market clearly understood this. The 80s saw titles change to financial planner and financial advisor, but advice was more a veneer for selling a product. The turn of the century saw the introduction of formal training requirements and legislation dictating how financial advice should be delivered. This produced a substantial shift from a product emphasis to advice. But even after the Global Financial Crisis you will still hear talk of sales targets, share of wallet, cross sales and activity metrics – particularly from the big end of town. Compliance is seen as an obstacle to doing business and additional legislation met with coordinated resistance. Is it any wonder that so many people question our priorities?

Trust requires a low S. To be perceived as trustworthy, we need to put our clients first and be able to enable our clients to understand this. How can this be achieved? By removing conflicts of interest, having a well-capitalised business and providing transparency.

Conflicts of interest

Self-orientation is challenged where conflicts of interest exist. A conflict of interest occurs where an advisor is presented with a choice between doing what is best for himself and what is best for a client. It is not a win-win scenario. Depending on the choice made, one party will benefit at the expense of the other. And the origin of almost each and every conflict is how an advisor will be paid for her services. Where a material part of an advisor's reward is linked in any way to a bonus for hitting a sales target or the type or amount of product sold to a client, a conflict exists. The conflict will exert even more influence on advisors who are under some form of financial pressure.

The only way to eliminate this conflict is to completely break the nexus between product and reward. That means adopting a pure fee for advice model. Where an advisor prices his fees purely on value drivers such as the complexity of a client's financial position (and the corresponding advice required) and the expertise and experience required to deliver this advice, all conflict is removed. Can an advisor over quote or misrepresent the work required? Sure, but this is an issue for the individual not the entire profession. It's specific, not systemic.

I have been challenged on several occasions with the argument that some clients, in fact, prefer an advisor's reward be linked to product performance. That where investments increase in value, an advisor should receive higher fees. Clients see this as the advisor having "skin in the game". I don't see it this way and I'll offer two reasons why:

- This arrangement ensures that the advisor receives higher fees in strong markets and lower fees in weaker markets. Yet our value to our clients is especially apparent during periods of market weakness. We tend to invest considerably more time with fearful clients who need to hear our perspective on the markets and who seek emotional support. The flip side is true during bull markets. Clients are patient, at peace and seldom seek our counsel. Receiving higher remuneration for less work and lower where we add greatest value is a warped model.

- This arrangement also misrepresents our role in wealth creation. I accept that there is a large part of the market for financial advice that confuses financial advisors with investment experts. They believe that the primary role of an advisor is to provide them with good investment returns (whatever that means). In Chapter 7 I'll go into some detail around where

I believe the value of financial advice sits and how to articulate your value in a compelling way. At this point I simply want to say that misrepresenting where our value lies by suggesting that we play an instrumental role in wealth creation – and are therefore happy to link our reward to the rise and fall of our client's funds – does us no favours.

Financial advice is certainly not the only profession that needs to address conflicts of interest. But because of our history and the unique qualities of financial advice (complexity, opacity, intangibility) we need to be especially sensitive to this issue.

Don't open up an undercapitalised business

If you're reading this book as a salaried advisor, take heed. One of the many attractions of becoming a financial advisor is the opportunity to be your own boss. This journey often starts off by working at a big institution or for a small practice. Whichever it is, working capital is not an issue for the salaried employee. Things change when you open your own shop. Suddenly there are bills to pay – even if you're a one-person show. Faced with this reality, it is only human to put your needs above those of your clients. You won't save yourself by promising to always put your clients first. You'll save yourself by ensuring that you start off with a well-capitalised business. This buys time. Having a financial runway ensures that you have the time to choose which clients you wish to work with and then to provide them with the services they truly need.

Transparency

I've mentioned several times the complexity associated with providing financial advice. Conflicts of interest can easily be concealed. When it comes to self-orientation, it is not good enough for you to do all the right things. Your client needs to understand how you've arranged your business in order to avoid conflicts of interest. They need to accept, to believe, that you really have their interests as your priority. Adopting a fee for advice model is the first step. Communicating this to your client is the next. By being transparent about why you charge your fees in a particular way and then providing your client with a fee schedule that exposes early in the engagement *how* you charge and *what* your actual fees are, you stamp out the concern that somehow this is all about you and your needs.

Final word

The need for a financial advisor to create trust and be thought of as trustworthy is clear cut. Clients will not engage with you, will not open up to you and will certainly not commit to doing business with you until they feel a certain level of trust in you. Some of this trust may be granted because of the brand you work within. You may receive a head start thanks to a referral from a trusted source. But for the majority of discerning clients who take their financial affairs seriously and who seek the ongoing counsel of a financial advisor, your credibility, your reliability, your ability to make people feel comfortable and at ease in your presence, and the transparency of your priorities, will dictate whether they lower their defences and open their heart and mind to what you have to say to them.

Key points from this chapter

- Trust is an important determinant of success. We will struggle to satisfy our client's thinking and move past Stage 1 of the cognitive map if we are unable to be perceived as worthy of their trust.

- Our profession has more headwinds in this regard than others. This is partly due to our history and partly due to the nature of financial advice itself.

- Maister, Green and Galford have provided us with a very powerful model that enables us to understand the components of trust and thus equip us with the insights necessary to present ourselves as being trustworthy. The model has four variables.

- The first variable in their model is credibility – how believable we are. We are able to build this in several ways.

- The second variable is reliability. We need to demonstrate this.

- The third variable is intimacy – how comfortable people feel in our presence. We need to be aware what influences this.

- The fourth variable is self-orientation – our priorities in the relationship. We need to develop a transparent business model that enables our client to understand how we provide value and how we are rewarded for doing this.

Chapter 3:

The power of framing

"If you had to identify, in one word, the reason why the human race has not achieved, and never will achieve, its full potential, that word would be 'meetings'."

Dave Berry
Author and winner of the Pulitzer Prize

I clearly remember one of my early conversations with a prospective client, but for all the wrong reasons. I'd recently completed my accounting articles and had set myself up as a financial advisor. After a few weeks of clumsy marketing I started to get a dribble of activity. My single-room office bragged a new cherry-wood meeting table with four fancy leather chairs and a small desk on which sat a desktop and a dot matrix printer. An older gent was comfortably seated on one of the leather chairs and I'd fixed him up with a glass of lukewarm water from the communal kitchen down the corridor from my office.

I instinctively sought to build rapport with a flow of small talk, all the while seeking an opportunity to cut to the chase of why he was here and what I could do for him. Like a saturated box of matches, the conversation just didn't seem to spark. We'd hit a good patch and then digress. We both seemed desperate for guidance. None came and an hour passed. He needed to leave for another appointment and I was thrilled to see him go, if only just to break the tension. We loosely agreed to meet again and pick up where we left off. Of course that was the last I saw of him.

On the disaster scale this meeting was about a nine out of ten. Even so, I reckon it's not that uncommon. Most new financial advisors and even a reasonable number of experienced advisors still struggle to get consistent shape and direction with their client meetings – particularly when meeting a prospective client for the first time.

The cognitive map helps us to understand what our clients are thinking. In the majority of cases they arrive at our offices cautious and wary. Those who have not worked with an advisor before have little idea of what to expect. They may have preconceptions, done a bit of homework perusing our website but, like anything new, there is an element of unease. You would have experienced this yourself when you arrived for your first day at a new employer. Or the first time you made a major presentation. Or the first time you donated blood. We fear the unknown. Even those who have received financial advice in the past will proceed carefully. The most likely reason why they are seeking your services is that they've had an unsatisfactory experience with their previous advisor.

Building trust and rapport in the way described in Chapter 2 will go a long way to reducing tension and even creating early client engagement and buy-in. There is one more exceptionally powerful concept that I'd like to share that will ensure that you are well prepared to guide your clients through Stage 1. That's the power of *framing*.

Framing

Framing enables you to create parameters for a discussion so that the conversation remains relevant and focused. Framing enables you to subtly set the agenda without your prospective client feeling disempowered or disrespected. Using a formal agenda when first meeting a person can leave them with a feeling of being corralled, disempowered and questioning your self-orientation. Meetings without an agenda introduce uncertainty and have an absence of clear purpose. Framing is a win-win technique. You provide direction for the meeting without leaving your client feeling herded.

Using this technique is simple. All that is required is for you to develop your own Statement of Intent (sometimes called an Agenda Statement). A Statement of Intent is simply that – what you believe the intent of the current meeting should be. You'll deliver this soon after the initial pleasantries have been exchanged and your client is sitting down wondering where the meeting will go and what will happen next. The impact of a well-structured and authentically-delivered statement is an immediate reduction of tension, a lift in your trustworthiness (via a reduction in perceived self-orientation) and a clarity of purpose for the meeting itself.

Developing your Statement of Intent

I'm going to provide you with a particularly good narrative from one of the most successful advisors I have ever had the opportunity to learn from. Andrew Watt explained that there were three parts to the Statement of Intent:

- Purpose – why are we here?
- Process – how this meeting is going to flow
- Benefit – what value you'll receive from this meeting

It should be short and crafted using words that you're comfortable with and would use in a normal conversation.

Here's a typical example of how Andrew uses this technique. He'll exchange pleasantries, often asking if they had any trouble finding his offices, making a remark about the weather, or perhaps a comment about the current headline of the day, and then, with an almost imperceptible pause, deliver his Statement of Intent:

> When I first meet a client, I like to seize the opportunity to ask several questions.
>
> This helps me to understand what you'd like to achieve, and allows me to consider whether I am able to deliver.
>
> It also gives you an opportunity to form an early impression of me.
>
> If I am able to add value, I would like to briefly discuss some possible solutions, and how my fees work.
>
> By the end of this meeting I'm confident that we'll both be clear on whether there's merit in us working together.
>
> Are you comfortable with this approach?

What would a client think after hearing this statement? Here are some possibilities:

- "I'm being respected. I've been asked for my permission for the meeting to take place in this way."
- "It's about me. This person doesn't seem to want to sell me something, but seems to want to genuinely understand what my needs are – and whether they can actually help."

- "They haven't made an assumption that I'm going to do business with them. They're giving me permission to form an opinion of them and then make a choice."
- "Phew! I now understand what this meeting is all about and I'm really comfortable with what this advisor has proposed."
- "Ah! He's going to let me know how much this will cost. I'll wait to hear what he suggests and then I'll decide whether it's worth it."

A fluent, authentic, well-delivered and well-timed Statement of Intent sets the agenda, relaxes and empowers your client and will enable you to achieve your objective far more consistently.

Going back to Andrew's Statement of Intent, although subtle, his objective is to get to a point in the meeting where he'll ask for the client's commitment to work with him. He's opened the door in an unthreatening way at the start of the conversation. His client has agreed to the agenda and won't resent being asked to commit because they have already agreed to this. Andrew has also shifted the pervasive question of costs to late in the meeting. This enables him to build value before discussing fees (more of this in Chapter 7).

What are we trying to accomplish here?

The Statement of Intent gives context to a meeting. It provides a mutually acceptable purpose for the meeting. Let me squeeze in a few ideas about meeting management in general that should constructively contribute to how you approach a meeting and how you measure the success or otherwise of that meeting.

People tend to be scathing towards meetings. I've spent my fair share of time in the corporate world attending five or more meetings a day, and occasionally, five-day meetings. There's seldom bang for your buck in this format. The talent to run an effective, productive meeting seems to be in the hands of a chosen few. It seems to me that the key ingredient missing from many meetings is a clear objective of what we want to accomplish at that meeting. An agenda is no substitute for a lack of a clear purpose. Some advisors walk into a meeting with no defined objective. With no specific objective you have nothing to aim at and certainly nothing to measure the success or otherwise of that meeting.

Having an objective is no guarantee of success. But it does lend focus and intent and you'll find yourself managing a meeting differently when you commit yourself to a particular objective, or, as I'm going to suggest, a key objective and a minimum objective.

Your key objective is your first prize. Andrew wants a commitment from his client to start the advice process rolling. He has a busy practice and little time for tyre-kickers and procrastinators. A client accepting the terms of his engagement and locking in a time to complete a Fact Find (or even doing it then and there if time permits) is his first prize. Andrew does realise though, that some people may not be able to make a commitment because they need to take some further action. This could involve consulting with a spouse or partner or getting input from another professional advisor (for example, their accountant) or finding out additional information. Gaining a client's commitment to this interim step – and locking in the next meeting – is Andrew's minimum objective. Either outcome is acceptable because he has met his objective. What's not acceptable to Andrew, and where he'd regard the meeting as a failure, is a prospective client who is unwilling to make a commitment and is vague about what his intentions are. Here, Andrew will crisply state that he understands that this person has chosen not do to business with him, that it has been a pleasure chatting, and he wishes them every success for the future. In this way Andrew does not allow himself to build a shopping list of possible clients that may make him complacent ("I've got a very full pipeline") and distract him from putting all his energies into clients who would benefit from his advice and who are seeking this.

Andrew is keenly aware of the difference between an "Advance" and a "Continuation" and I'd like you to be alert to this too.

Advances and Continuations

There are hundreds, perhaps thousands of books on sales skills. For the skills and insights required to sell financial advice, one stands head and shoulders above the rest – Neil Rackham's unfortunately named book *SPIN Selling*. The word "spin" is usually associated with bending the truth and twisting the facts. This book has nothing to do with any sort of twisting or manipulation and "SPIN" is in fact an acronym that offers us particularly useful guidance for developing and asking questions. I'll be discussing how we can benefit from this unique approach in the next chapter.

The part of *SPIN Selling* that is of importance to us here is Rackham's comments around meetings – what constitutes a successful meeting and what should be considered a failure. In SPIN, Rackham differentiates between a "simple" sale and a "complex" sale. A simple sale usually involves a single engagement between buyer and seller. I pop into a bookshop and peruse the business book section. An assistant sidles up and offers assistance. I explain what I'm looking for and she makes a few suggestions. One hits the spot and I buy the book. This is a successful simple sale. It's binomial: either the single meeting – in this case on the floor of a bookshop – will produce a sale or it won't. A complex sale involves several goals, a number of considerations, often multiple decision makers and, more often than not, multiple meetings. Limited or tightly-scoped advice – for example, buying personal insurance when taking out a mortgage – may be a simple sale. Customised, holistic advice would almost always be considered a complex sale. It is just this expectation of multiple meetings that traps the unwary advisor into investing considerable time and effort in meetings with clients who won't choose to proceed at some point.

Rackham describes an Advance as a meeting where something takes place "that moves the sale (conversation) forward toward a decision".[10] An Advance is not necessarily closing, it is making constructive progress. A Continuation occurs "where no specific action has been agreed upon by the customer to move it forward".[11]

When you enter a meeting knowing what your primary and minimum objectives are, you position yourself to deliver an appropriate Statement of Intent, to give direction to the meeting where required and to pull the plug whenever you experience a Continuation. It is this awareness that ensures all meetings have purpose but that only some meetings should be considered successful and further time invested with that particular prospective client.

Statements of Control

Statements of Control are used to get conversations back on track. The more we allow the conversation to digress, the less chance we have of securing an Advance. A Statement of Control enables you to halt and reset the direction a conversation is taking. Let me illustrate this principle with two examples:

Your prospective client is finding it difficult to explain his current position and the meeting is losing momentum and direction. You could use a Statement of Control like, "Let's pause here for a moment. I'd like to make sure that I've understood how you're seeing your financial situation." You could then play the conversation back to your client in a tighter, more articulate way.

You'll introduce clarity, rescue the meeting and reset its direction.

Your prospective client wants to understand how much you charge. It's early in the meeting and you have had little opportunity to understand her circumstances and therefore have little idea about what advice you will be able to provide. You could make the fatal error of discussing your fees before you have even exposed her needs and discussed some potential courses of action. Or you could take control of the conversation with a Statement of Control like, "I have no idea at this stage what my fees will be. I'm not even clear on what you are looking to achieve and whether I'll be able to assist. I'm comfortable that towards the end of our meeting I'll have a much better understanding and will discuss my fees then."

Final word

Financial advisors have no toolbox, no machinery which manufactures our advice and no fleet of trucks to deliver this. We work with words and the emotions contained in those words and the mood that surrounds those words. Most of our best work takes place in the meeting room. Our ability to engage our clients in this environment, to gently direct conversations so that prospective clients are encouraged to seek our services, and so that maximum value is enjoyed by our current clients, is a key determinant of the degree of success we will experience in this emerging profession.

Key points from this chapter

- Framing enables you to create parameters for a discussion so that the conversation remains relevant and focused. You are able to frame a conversation with a Statement of Intent.
- There are three parts to a Statement of Intent: purpose, process and benefit.
- You should enter each and every meeting you attend with a key objective and a minimum objective. Failure to achieve your minimum objective means ceasing to invest any further time with that prospective client.
- A complex sales meeting can either end as an Advance or a Continuation. An Advance occurs when there has been some form of constructive progress. A Continuation occurs when there has been none. Do not schedule a further meeting when the current meeting has ended as a Continuation.
- A Statement of Control allows you to keep meetings on track and provides you with a better chance of securing an Advance.

Chapter 4:

The power of questions

"Questions have great power. One right question asked at the right time can change the direction of our lives. Hence, the quality of the questions that we ask ourselves is very important."

Rajesh Setty

Entrepreneur, Author, Speaker and Alchemist

There's a joke told about Albert Einstein during his days as a university professor. Einstein submitted the year-end exam paper to his colleagues for their review and comment. They were surprised to discover that this year's questions were exactly the same as the previous year's questions. Thinking the mighty Professor Einstein had tried to sneak one past them, they challenged him. To which Einstein replied, "You are correct! This year's questions are the same as last year's. But the answers have changed." There's a much deeper meaning to this very simple joke…

As kids our thoughts flow freely. Kids don't have preconceptions. They see the world as it is. You'd have heard the saying, "Out of the mouths of babes comes truth." As we grow older we start to define ourselves and develop firm ideas about who we are and how the world works. This process continues throughout our lives and that's why older people tend to be much more conservative and fixed in the way they see and do things. As we age, we become less and less able to perceive and consider alternate viewpoints and explore other possibilities. It's not as though we become narrow minded and unwilling to do so. It's just that we are not able to. Our natural evolution is to "own" who we are and live our lives according to the rules we've developed for ourselves. In fact, the impact of this fixed thinking on the quality of our lives has spawned the massive self-improvement industry and has made celebrities of the likes of Anthony Robbins, Wayne Dyer, Jack Canfield and many others. Every self-improvement guru pedals the same message: your life can be so much better than the one you're living now. Seeing a better future for ourselves is a thrilling feeling.

While Robbins, Dyer, Canfield et al have the brand and the visibility, it's in fact the financial advisor who is presented with the ongoing opportunity. As a financial advisor, you help your client define their goals. You hold their hand over the years, encouraging them to stay in the game and see their financial plan to fruition.

You are there to provide the ongoing support and encouragement needed for them to actually make their life better, rather than just temporarily spiking their enthusiasm with a book, video or event.

And the catalyst, the enabler to achieve this, is the well-crafted question.

I'm raising the bar in this chapter. My challenge to you is not to just master the power of questions but to use this enabling skill to unlock the minds of the people you meet, the people who seek your advice and to give them a peek of wonderful possibilities they never before considered. Think big. Some questions can result in tax being saved. Some questions can result in lives being changed.

Instant benefits of asking questions

Most people would suggest the purpose of asking a question is to elicit information. Many of the sales courses that I've attended made this presumption and approach questions in a structural way.

What didn't get too much coverage were insights on why great questions produce amazing results, how to fashion these questions and when to use them. These insights came later through trial and error, observing others, and through the magic of Neil Rackham's SPIN.

I now appreciate that there are far higher purposes and substantial benefits for asking great questions. I'd like to share three:

Questions enable you to build rapport

It's only natural in a conversation that the person who asks the questions does much less talking than the person answering. In an earlier chapter I discussed the impact that being listened to has on a person. As Dale Carnegie says, "Listening is one of the highest compliments we can pay anyone."[12] The Greek philosopher Epictetus said "We have two ears and one mouth so that we can listen twice as much as we speak." Asking questions is superb meeting management. It gets your prospective client to talk and provides you with an opportunity to listen and thus build rapport.

Questions enable you to build trust

Have you ever had the feeling that you haven't been understood correctly? You're giving a food order at a restaurant and requesting a few changes to the standard fare. The waiter nods a lot, scribbles furiously – and then heads off to the kitchen to place the order. And you wonder, "Jeez, I hope he got that right." You're sitting in front of your doctor. She asks a few questions and then makes a diagnosis and you think, "That was a bit quick. I'm not sure I explained exactly how I'm feeling and where it hurts." Thorough, probing questions build trust. We are left with a sense that the person who will guide us fully understands what we want to achieve and we will therefore have more trust in the appropriateness of the solution they propose.

Questions engage emotions

The saying "People buy with their hearts, not their minds" is attributed to many people. That's not surprising because it's such a perceptive observation. As much as we'd like to bluff ourselves that we make important decisions in a cold, calculating and logical manner, we don't. While our mind grapples with a torrent of features, benefits, permutations, trade-offs and possibilities, our gut sends a clear signal – "run away", or "go for it". Sure, we rationalise afterwards. "That was a really good idea because yada, yada, yada…" But almost always we go by gut instinct. Constructing great questions enables us to engage with our prospective clients on an emotional level. Trust and rapport opens the mind. Great questions engage with the heart.

Questions and the cognitive map

Before I discuss how to create your own great questions – and share a few of the best I've encountered – let's reflect on the cognitive map which describes your client's journey from cautious and defensive to committed and engaged. Stage 1 – the start of the meeting – usually sees a client's mind in a defensive position. There's the natural emotional polarity that exists when people meet for the first time in a situation where one seeks to influence the other. Questions are an exceptionally effective way to create both trust and rapport by providing you with the opportunity to show interest in your client (lowers self-orientation by communicating that the meeting is about them and their needs) and to listen while your client speaks (increasing intimacy by demonstrating courtesy and respect). Trust is further enhanced as your client believes that – through your questions – you fully understand their circumstances and needs and will therefore deliver an appropriate solution.

Questions enable you to guide your client's mind through Stage 2 where you are required to gently challenge your client's status quo. People own their decisions, for better or for worse. Constructing and employing great questions causes your client to reflect on where they are and to come to their own conclusions about whether they wish to make changes. Your ability to disturb and create emotional angst, or to excite and provide emotional desire, rests in the quality of the questions you ask. Expect great resistance when you directly challenge your client's perceptions and beliefs with statements. You will not progress through Stage 2 and you may very well undo all the good work you've done to progress through Stage 1. Where you enable your client to reflect on their circumstances and to come to their own conclusions, they are absolutely on board with you.

How to craft great questions

I introduced you to Neil Rackham's "SPIN" in the previous chapter. We spoke about the concept of "Advances" and "Continuations" in the context of meeting management. For financial advisors, Rackham's most valuable contribution is to provide us with a philosophy to both create and employ great questions. SPIN introduces four types of questions that not only get a client to talk to us, but to sell to themselves at the same time.

I'm going to quickly run through the theory and then provide examples of how you can use Rackham's SPIN in practice.

SPIN – the theory

"SPIN" is an acronym for four types of questions – Situation, Problem, Implication and Need-payoff. We ask these questions in that order too.

Situation Questions are the typical questions that you'd ask in a Fact Find. Situation questions are designed to obtain facts – how old are you, how much do you earn, have you got life insurance, what is the balance of your retirement fund, etc. These are the bread and butter questions of every financial advisor. Situation Questions simply extract content from your prospective client. Whatever you've asked the client *already knows*.

This brings Rackham to make two interesting observations: "Buyers quickly become bored or impatient if asked too many Situation Questions"[13] and that "inexperienced salespeople ask more Situation Questions than those with greater selling experience" presumably "because Situation Questions are easy to ask and they feel safe".[14]

In my work with financial advisors I observe that the majority ask almost exclusively Situation Questions. Without knowing it, we are boring prospective clients by extracting information that our clients already know. While we need to get this information as it is critical to providing advice, the mistake made by many is to stop asking questions at this point and to start providing high level solutions. If we do this our prospective client's thinking remains becalmed in Stage 2. They have provided us with their point of view. They are thinking "I'm okay". By simply extracting objective facts we have left them behind in this mindset while we move ahead to discuss the benefits of working with us (Stage 3) and the specifics of what we can do for them (Stage 4).

We need to challenge our clients' views of the world. We need to gently help them to become aware that things are not okay. We do this by asking Problem Questions.

Problem Questions probe for "problems, difficulties, or dissatisfactions".[15] Having gathered factual information you are now in a position to identify problems and weaknesses in your client's current position.

So a Situation Question might be "How are your superannuation funds currently invested?" This question simply seeks facts – are your funds in cash, in managed funds, direct equities, etc.?

By contrast, a Problem Question is "What thought have you given to how you've invested your funds?" This question uncovers potential issues (most often there has been very little thought given or none at all).

Good Problem Questions enable our clients to view their decisions and circumstances in a fresh way. These sorts of questions create value and purpose by helping the prospective client to begin to understand where the value in a relationship with you lies. It's not about what you want to sell them; it's about what they need. You develop their awareness of their needs by asking well-crafted Problem Questions.

All selling needs to disturb or inspire; Problem Questions are designed to disturb. We need to engage with our clients on an emotional level because it is emotions, not facts, that motivate action. Going back to the 70s and Shultz's sizzling sausages, I used to love listening to the life agents' and brokers' alcohol-oiled stories of client conquest. Their one-liners that supposedly had clients scrambling for a pen to sign a life app, "He kept knocking me back. And then I saw him with his kids at school sports and I went up to him and said, 'look at your kids. Where will they be if you got hit by a bus tomorrow?'" Some were a bit more subdued, "So what keeps you awake at night?" These are examples of the classic disturb questions from the time when sideburns were very long and people smoked on planes. But today, these disturb tactics would be regarded as tacky, damaging to the gravitas of the professional and, frankly, lacking in integrity. I say lacking in integrity because to me, to disturb with no other purpose than to sell lacks integrity. I remember the angst a real estate agent's disturb question caused my mother-in-law. She'd just sold her house and was taking her time looking for a smaller property. The agent, keen to accelerate the process asked, "Aren't you worried that the market's going to run away from you?" Problem Questions are linked to the facts that emerge from asking Situation Questions.

They are not emotional bayonets to expedite a sale by panicking a client. In this way they have integrity and can be comfortably used by the professional financial advisor.

Problem Questions challenge and unsettle a client's complacency and commitment to their status quo. Implication Questions are designed to continue this mental journey.

Implication Questions are designed to help your client explore the consequences of their problems. Motivating a client to take action often needs more than just helping then to identify problems and opportunities – it needs your client to feel a powerful emotional desire sufficient to overcome the natural tendency to procrastinate and live with a subpar solution. Implication Questions move the mind from thinking, "I do have a problem, but I can live with it", to "Dammit. This is serious. I need to fix this."

Again, let me provide clarity by expanding the example I used for Problem Questions.

Problem Question: "What thought have you given to how you've invested your funds?" If your client answers "very little" (as is often the case), your next questions could be:

Implication Question: "Have you considered the possibility that your funds may be invested in completely the wrong assets?" or "Could it be that you are risking your retirement by not ensuring your money is appropriately invested?"

Let me stop here and make a few points:

1. The integrity of our questioning is sound. We are not badgering our client with questions we hope will disturb just for the sake of disturbing, but questions we expect will assist in making better decisions.

2. We are asking questions for which we will be able to provide appropriate solutions. Again, these aren't random hit-or-miss sales questions, they are carefully-crafted questions that are relevant to our client's needs and to which we are able to provide appropriate solutions. For both Implication Questions we will be able to model the classic four trade-offs of financial advice (current fund value, expected date of retirement, expected future contributions, and current asset allocation) and provide our client with valuable insights. We are not suggesting in any way that the current asset allocation is wrong. We are suggesting that because our client has given little or no thought to her current asset allocation that she is running the risk of a severely underfunded retirement.

SPIN joins the dots. We move our client from the facts of their situation to its consequences. It's easy to see how the use of Problem and Implication Questions enables us to move our client past the hurdle presented in Stage 2 – our need to challenge their complacency and to motivate them to take action.

The final letter of SPIN closes the loop.

Need-payoff Questions contain a solution but require the client to explain how the proposed solution would benefit them. They get your client to tell you the benefits of addressing the problem that was discovered in an earlier question. Before I provide an example, I want to consider how effective this type of question would be in moving your client's mind past Stage 3. It's at this stage where a client owns their problems and is considering whether to do something about them, but where they are not sure if it's worth the effort and whether you are the right person to work with. A great Need-payoff Question addresses both obstructions by presenting an acceptable (high level) solution and indicating that you would be the best person to proceed with. Why? Because you've just suggested a constructive course of action for a problem that is now causing some distress. Again, let me provide an example using our growing conversation above:

Problem Question: "What thought have you given to how you've invested your funds?"

Implication Question: "Could it be that you are risking your retirement by not ensuring your money is appropriately invested?"

Need-payoff Question: "Is it important to you to solve this problem?" or "Is this something you'd like an expert opinion on?"

Let your client now do the selling ...

Bringing it all together

You're sitting in front of a young couple who've just bought their first home and been lumbered with their first mortgage. From the Situation Questions you've established that the wife is pregnant (fact) and that they both believe they have adequate life insurance (perception) and aren't sure what you can offer. They're just here because their accountant – who they trust – suggested that they see you.

Advisor: You mentioned that you're both comfortable with the level of insurance you have now. How did you initially decide on this amount of insurance? [Problem]

Husband: We didn't really work out a specific number, we just felt a big amount like a million dollars each would be enough.

Advisor: Did you factor in taking out a mortgage at the time? [Problem]

Wife: Yes. That's why we've taken out such a big amount.

Advisor: What would the impact be if it turned out that your cover was much less than was actually needed? [Implication]

Husband: Well, it would be devastating if that was the case and something happened to me.

Advisor: If that were the case would you (looking at the wife) choose to sell and move into a smaller house? [Implication] Or perhaps move in with your folks? [Implication]

Wife: I really wouldn't want to think of that. I don't really like either possibility.

Advisor: Is this something you'd like me to provide advice on? So that you can get some certainty with this? [Need payoff]

I've addressed the common problem of people believing that they have enough insurance when they have made no effort to establish whether this is true or not. This complacency has ensured that much of the market remains woefully underinsured. You could take a very similar approach by querying whether your prospective client has considered whether they will be able to afford future premiums (many people take out stepped premium cover which they believe is more affordable), whether they have determined that they have the appropriate types of insurances (many people see insurance as one solution rather than several solutions for the different risks that we all face), and whether they have given any thought to how best they could structure their insurance to minimise tax and to protect proceeds from creditors or irresponsible (or simply inexperienced) beneficiaries.

Until you've mastered the enabling skill of SPIN selling I suggest that you jot down a few ideas for each of the four types of questions and have these on hand during client meetings. You'll soon find yourself adopting the SPIN flow and you'll begin crafting and employing great questions in real time.

While Neil Rackham's SPIN offers us a validated structure to create and apply questions to our circumstances, another extremely useful approach to using questions to develop rapport, build trust and create the emotion required for action is Dan Sullivan's DOS Conversation.

Dan's DOS

Dan Sullivan is the founder of an organisation called *Strategic Coach*. He describes his business as "an organisation run by entrepreneurs for entrepreneurs".[16] Self-employed advisors are a classic example of an entrepreneurial professional and Sullivan has a strong focus on developing solutions for our market. He's got a bit of a cult following and every year dozens of advisors from around the world jump onto planes and travel to far-flung Canada to attend one of his intensive retreats.

Sullivan's "DOS Conversation" is an ingenious and fresh approach that can be brought to how we engage with our prospective clients with the intention of securing their business.

I'd describe the DOS Conversation as a modified corporate SWOT* analysis that challenges the prospective client (and existing clients as well) to consider issues of particular personal importance. You'll have noticed that we're playing with acronyms in this chapter – "DOS" stands for Danger, Opportunity and Strength. These topics force the conversation to take both a personal and emotional shape. Remember, we get our prospective client's permission to ask these sorts of questions when we set the agenda through our Statement of Intent. We've got permission to ask questions. We must make absolutely sure that we use this opportunity to become informed, to engage, to become trusted and to motivate action.

---

* SWOT analysis (Strengths Weaknesses Opportunities Threats) is a strategic and tactical analysis tool often employed in corporate planning.

To start the DOS Conversation, try Sullivan's segue:

> *"If we were having this discussion three years from today, and you were looking back over those three years, what has to have happened in your life, both personally and professionally, for you to feel happy with your progress?"*[17]

And after the segue, straight into the "Dan Sullivan Question" itself, which forms the basis of the DOS Conversation:

> *"Specifically, what **dangers** do you have now that need to be eliminated, what **opportunities** need to be captured, and what **strengths** need to be maximised?"*[18]

From a technique perspective I would be sitting next to my client, not across a table or desk; or in front of a whiteboard. I'd mark three columns on the paper or board, insert the three headings, and let my prospective client talk to their heart's content.

What do we expect to achieve with this question?

When we ask people which **dangers** they believe they are exposed to, say within the next three years, we help them to articulate their fears. Our objective is to get them to look at themselves and their world in a way they seldom would and thereby produce insights that may have remained undiscovered – and most likely not attended to – if not for the time they've invested in meeting you. It's amazing how we welcome the opportunity to share our deepest thinking with a trusted, objective stranger. There will be personal revelations like health fears, financial worries, and relationship issues. You will also hear all sorts of misconceptions about investments and wealth creation. Fears that have caused them to remain in cash until things were just too rosy to stay on the sidelines, so they bought high, and then fears that made them sell low when the news was darkest. Fears that the system is gamed and that the ordinary guy never has a chance. There's a beautiful question in Dr Spencer Johnson's book, *Who Moved My Cheese?*, that asks, "What would you do if you weren't afraid?" You have positioned yourself to help your client explore this question in a very practical way.

When we ask people about which **opportunities** they seek to capture, we introduce excitement into the conversation. You will hear about dreams of a private education for their children, a longed-for sabbatical, a desire to study further, ambitions that reach to the top of the corporate ladder, early retirement, working a four-day week, purchasing a business.

You may hear about fears and dreams that have not been shared with close friends or spouses. So why open up to you? Because you've created a safe opportunity to do so. Because you have asked a great question that has motivated this much deeper and considered thinking. Because maybe you are just the right person to make it all happen.

When we ask people about their **strengths** we help them build confidence. We create energy and an opportunity to positively reflect on themselves (an experience that each of us should do far more often to reinforce our own self-worth). Many people take their talents, skills, experience, achievements, networks and other resources for granted. Our aim here is to raise our client's awareness and to support them to identify which resources need to be brought into play to eliminate, or at least manage, the dangers and which resources can be called out to provide the best chance of converting opportunities.

Once you have recorded each danger, opportunity and strength, Sullivan suggests that you ask your client to identify the top three in each column. Which three dangers do they fear the most? Which three opportunities are they hell bent on converting? Which three strengths make them feel most capable, most powerful? Finally you ask your client to prioritise each from one to three. These now become the goals for the work you'll do together.

The DOS Conversation is a wonderful solution for helping your client's mind move through Stages 2 and 3. The conversation enables your prospective client to come to their own conclusion that their current situation is not optimal and forcefully positions you as the right person with whom to tackle the new journey.

Unlike the SPIN model, which can be used in almost every conversation, the DOS Conversation is not particularly suitable for clients seeking a solution for an issue that requires a limited scope, the more transactional engagement. But people seeking a strategy, a plan and a relationship will be thrilled with this approach. It provides these types of clients with a structured opportunity to capture their thinking about issues that are important to them. It seems to me that many people live their lives with little thought and contemplation. By applying the DOS Conversation you provide a very valuable experience.

A plethora of great questions ... *

SPIN and DOS are great models. But if you're just on the lookout for some great questions that will equip you to lead your client's mind through the hurdles presented by Stages 1 and 2 of the cognitive map, here are some of the best that I've jotted down ...

Questions to build rapport

- "Most Australians aren't as financially successful as they should be. Why do you think this is so?" [There's no particular answer here. This question gets your client talking and allows you to get an idea of where they're coming from]
- "Tell me about yourself"
- "On a scale of 1 to 10, how comfortable are you with your financial affairs? _____, why do you say that?"
- "How many of your financial goals did you achieve last year?" [Helps understand if client a) sets goals and b) was successful in achieving them]

---

* I must credit Andrew Watt who I introduced in the previous chapter for sharing many of these questions with me. He uses these to superb effect and I know that he'll be pleased that others in our profession will be using his work to serve more people who desperately need advice and yet often lack the commitment required to implement our guidance.

- "Do you know the three biggest mistakes Australians make when it comes to investing?" [Again, no particular answer. Gets your client thinking and talking]

Questions that make effective meetings*

- "Are there any areas of concern that you would like to discuss today?"
- "Have you had the opportunity to work with a financial advisor before?"
- "What motivated you to meet with me today?"
- "What do we need to focus on today that's relevant to your needs?"
- "What are your expectations of me and our meeting today?" [Use to create agenda]

Questions to guide your client past Stage 2**

- "What thought have you given to a situation where you weren't able to ...?"
- Questions that test feelings. "How would you feel ...?"
- "What consideration have you given to ...?"
- "What has been your experience with ...?"
- "How's it working?"
- "What makes you think that way?"
- "What qualities do you look for in ...?"
- "How do you see this working for you?"

---

* I still recommend that you develop and use a Statement of Intent. If you prefer to use questions to give shape and purpose to your meeting, these questions will do the trick.

** Many of these questions are in fact "Problem Questions" as defined in Rackham's SPIN model.

- "How do you determine.../How have you determined...?"
- "What are you doing differently this year to make sure that doesn't happen again?"
- "How do you go about making important financial decisions?"
- "Many Australians don't take the time to think through their financial position. How much time do you invest?"
- "What/who has been your trusted sources of advice/ guidance to date?"
- "What principles and values have you followed with money and investing?"
- "What's your philosophy for investing money?"
- "What are your strongest beliefs about money?"
- "What's your view on insurance?"
- "What good or bad experiences have occurred in your life regarding money and investing?"

Questions to obtain an Advance
(to make constructive progress)

- "You need to decide whether this is important to you. And whether I'm the right person to work with." [Statement asked as a question]
- "Is there anyone else's financial future that hinges on our conversation today?" OR "How will the decision to proceed be made?" [Uncovers all decision makers]
- "I'm comfortable that I'll be able to do all this. Before I outline my fees, would you like me to explain where we go from here?"

- "Are you comfortable to proceed on this basis?"
- "Would you like me to get things going?"
- "We've covered a lot of ground today. What specific area is causing you concern?"

Final word

A financial advisor is in many ways more a coach than a technician. We don't so much fix things as provide support for an important journey. We are not in the business of delivering dreams because we work with people with finite resources. We are in the best position to challenge the limits of our client's current thinking and in that way enable them to look at their life from a fresh perspective and to discover opportunities and outcomes they would otherwise never have imagined. Our role is to then craft a plan that will give them the best chance of success and to provide them with the motivation and discipline that each and every worthwhile endeavour requires.

Key points from this chapter

- Well-crafted questions have three substantial benefits:
  - They enable you to build rapport,
  - They enable you to build trust, and
  - They ensure that the conversation takes place on both logical and emotional levels.
- SPIN is a philosophy to create and employ great questions:
  - Situation Questions are designed to obtain facts,
  - Problem Questions probe for difficulties and weaknesses,
  - Implication Questions help explore the consequences of your client's problems, and
  - Need-payoff Questions require your client to explain how a proposed solution would benefit them.
- The DOS Conversation is a conversation based on a single question. It provides a framework that challenges your client to consider issues of personal importance. In particular, what dangers they believe they are exposed to, what opportunities they seek to capture and what resources they are able to contribute to combating the dangers they wish to avoid and opportunities they wish to seize.

Chapter 5:

Weapons of influence – the psychology of persuasion

"Those that will not hear must be made to feel"

German proverb

It happened a long time ago on a rugby field far, far away ...

The year was 1995 and South Africa was hosting the Rugby Union World Cup. It was a time of great tension and uncertainty for the country. The previous year had seen the change in government from white minority rule to full democracy and the predominantly black ANC as the country's ruling party. The white community felt uncertain, disempowered, marginalised and fearful for the future.

The final game of the competition was played between the mighty New Zealand All Blacks – the most consistently successful team of the modern rugby era – and South Africa's Springboks. The game was to be played at Ellis Park in Johannesburg. For white South Africans, rugby was a sport that expressed passion and power. The Springbok was a symbol of excellence; of success over many decades. For the black majority, the Springbok was a reminder of oppression, of white domination. Many felt that the symbol should be banned from all sporting codes and, in fact, rugby was the last sport to use the leaping antelope.

The local team had reached the finals against all expectations. The Springboks had returned from nearly two decades of official isolation only three years previously. There was a wonderful mood among the overwhelmingly white crowd. All the country's problems seemed far away on that crisp, clear winter afternoon. The crowd's excitement surged when a Boeing 747 flew low over the stadium. The kick-off was only minutes away.

And then an incredible thing happened. The steady buzz of thousands of pre-game conversations started to fade. It paused and an unnatural silence settled on the stadium. Everyone's attention was focused on the player's tunnel. For out of this tunnel walked a man. South Africa's new president – Nelson Mandela. But it wasn't the president that was the source of excited whispers that were growing louder by the second. It was what he was wearing.

As he emerged from the shadows of the tunnel under the main stand, it became clear that the man who was imprisoned for twenty-seven years and who was now the country's first black president was wearing a Springbok rugby jersey.

The crowd's joy was overwhelming. In one simple gesture Mandela had communicated to the 80,000 white fans in the stadium – and the five million watching on television – that not only were they forgiven, but that he was prepared to embrace a symbol hated by blacks, revered by whites.

On that day white and black South Africans shared common ground as never before. The stadium erupted. The buzz turned into a chant. Conservative white South Africans – no friend of Mandela or the ANC – chanted "Mandela, Mandela, Mandela!" with passion and joy and love.

What I didn't understand then, but what I understand now, is the psychology behind the white community's response to Mandela's action. It was much more than the bond that sports fans feel to others wearing their team's colours. It was much more than being forgiven or of being accepted by a foe now turned friend. It was a realisation that the perceived foe may have, in fact, been a friend all along. Mandela used a weapon of influence as a force for good, an opportunity to reconcile, an opportunity to dissolve fear, an opportunity to build trust. That simple gesture, that masterly use of influence as a force for good, is a moment that I will always treasure.

The psychology of persuasion

If Nelson Mandela can use the psychology of persuasion to sell the New South Africa to its white minority, then it has much use for us too. Make no mistake. This was a hard sell. After decades of privilege the white psyche was mired in Stage 2 – I'm okay. I don't want to change. I'm not buying what you have to sell, Mr Mandela. In 1995, White South Africa demonstrated all the wariness, the stubbornness, the resistance to change to their new government that often characterises the mindset of those we sit down with for the first time. We need to equip ourselves appropriately to work with the stubborn and the headstrong and the overconfident. At times we need to be armed with weapons of influence. And that's just what this chapter is all about.

The psychology of persuasion is now a mainstream branch of psychology. It seeks to understand why we respond so consistently when presented with certain scenarios. It has allowed us to understand that some of our brain is simply hardwired to behave in certain ways. That much of human behaviour can be strongly influenced when carefully chosen words push our prehistoric hot buttons. That our logical modern minds can be short-circuited and that our response is influenced by synapses configured eons ago.

As we move through this chapter I will share not just the principles involved in the psychology of persuasion, but their ancient origin and how we can best apply them in our current work. My objective is to present you with weapons of influence that will enable you to take on and motivate action with your toughest prospective clients.

Use with care

There is no licence required to arm one's self with these weapons. There should be. When reading this chapter you'll recognise how others who have mastered this psychology have used their skills to manipulate rather than to influence. The dividing line here is intent. I see manipulation as self-serving, practised by those with a high self-orientation and therefore people who can and should be regarded as untrustworthy. I see influence as a necessary skill for the financial advisor. We face headwinds that other professions just don't have to work through. Our advice is complex, intangible and often the benefits of our guidance only manifest years after we first meet with our prospective client. Our market is continually reminded of our mixed history by both government and media, who present themselves as supposedly looking after the interests of the weak and gullible. We often work with people who have low financial literacy, limited understanding of what constitutes financial advice, a poor appreciation of their own financial position and a low level of interest. We need to be equipped with every possible skill that will enable us to connect, engage and thus motivate action. I regard the mastery of influence as a necessity for the financial advisor to do good.

Cialdini's brilliance

There are many great books on the topic of the psychology of persuasion. I referred to one such book, *The Power of Influence*, by my mentor Tom Lambert in Chapter 1. I have little hesitation in saying that the most accomplished writer and the person from whom I have gained the bulk of my insights is Professor Robert Cialdini, who operates out of Arizona State University. His book *Influence, The Psychology of Persuasion*, is simply a must-read on this topic. I will use his six principles as the foundation for this chapter and simply provide ideas for the practical use of each in context of the advisor-client conversation.

Cialdini's six principles of persuasion are: reciprocation, consistency, social proof, liking, scarcity and authority (credibility).

Principle One: Reciprocation – People have a natural urge to reciprocate a kind deed

> *"Give a little bit,*
> *Give a little bit of your love to me*
> *I'll give a little bit*
> *I'll give a little bit of my love to you."*
> Supertramp
> *Even in the Quietest Moments* (1977)

Many millennia ago, as bearskin-clad Neanderthals, we needed reciprocation to survive. If I returned from a hunt empty handed, I needed to count on you for food that evening. You'd share your spoils with me, not because you were generous by nature, but because you knew that you'd also experience an unsuccessful hunt some day and would then come knocking on my cave. Reciprocation increased our chances of survival.

We live in less dramatic times. But our reptilian brains still respond instinctively to certain stimuli. When I buy you a coffee you instinctively offer to buy me one at the next opportunity. You'll say "It's my shout", or words to that effect.

This instinctive impulse works all the time. At a pub you buy a round of drinks and others will reciprocate by buying the next round. Smile at someone walking past and they'll smile back. You've dined at a friend's house and you'll soon be looking for an opportunity to invite them over to yours.

Why are fund managers and insurers so generous with their cash? How many Christmas parties, breakfasts, golf days, sports events and conferences have you been invited to? How many golf balls, movie tickets and assorted pens and paraphernalia have you received from Business Development Managers and – if you're a heavy hitter – more senior management?

Each and every gift, each and every invitation builds up a small emotional debt in the recipient. Try as you might, it's very hard to remain objective. You feel a deep primeval need to clear the debt. To reciprocate. The urge is so strong that legislation was introduced to limit the quantum of the gifts and benefits a financial advisor can receive.

My mate Harold is a master of using the principle of reciprocation. He's a self-employed consultant who works with businesses looking to grow their top line. He also does a lot of keynote speaking. He'd heard about a particular event and was very keen to be involved. He met with the Managing Director of the company hosting the event and was told that he was up against a handful of other speakers. After a few minutes he discovered that the MD was newly appointed and that the conference for which he was interviewing speakers was his first major event at the company. The MD also had limited experience in arranging these kinds of events and was relying heavily on his, as yet untested, personal assistant. The company's national sales force was to be flown in and he wanted to make an excellent first impression.

Harold looked the MD in the eye and said "Look. I've been involved in many conferences like yours. If you're free later this week I'll pick you up and show you some of the better venues and share some ideas that have had a great impact." The MD accepted the offer.

It was then extremely difficult not to invite Harold to speak. An emotional debt has been created and reciprocation was required. Harold got the gig.

Practical ways to use this principle

Look for an opportunity to give. Not something crass like a branded pen or something extravagant that can be misconstrued as a bribe. Here are some ideas:

- Send your prospective client a newspaper clipping or website link that is related to something that she expressed an interest in when you met. It could be some information that she was looking for or something interesting about a hobby of hers.

Look through the notes you took during your first conversation and you'll find many opportunities.

- Give him a book that again is connected to something he told you about, something he expressed an interest in. Books are great gifts. They are seen as both a present and a desire to contribute to the recipient's knowledge. Be sure to make a hand-written note inside. It personalises the gift even more.

- I'm a natural linker. I always look for opportunities to introduce people who share a common interest or common objective. If your prospective client is in business and you feel confident in doing so, look to make introductions that will benefit both parties. Look for opportunities to refer business their way. "I've got a client who owns a dozen milkshake kiosks. He's looking for new suppliers at the moment. Can I ask him to get in touch with you?"

- Finally, give them a concession. If they want to meet after hours or at a venue that doesn't suit you, tell them that you usually don't work those hours because you have committed the time to exercise or family. But for them you are willing to make an exception. Same with having to travel when you prefer not to. Don't lose this opportunity by downplaying the extra effort you are going to. "Well, I don't usually work that way. But if it's important to you …"

Principle Two: Consistency – People have an inbuilt desire to be consistent

People like to appear consistent. People who are consistent are admired. "You always know where you stand with Brad", "Jacky is very reliable. You can always count on her."

Like many of these principles, our need to be consistent dates back to primeval times. We needed clarity to know what was good and what was bad. Who was a friend and who was the enemy. Who to trust and who to run from. We need to feel that people in government, commerce and other areas that have an impact on our lives are going to act in a consistent manner. When they don't, we often experience great discomfort. There is a psychological comfort associated with the status quo, while change tends to introduce angst and discomfort.

Most people don't change sports teams just because their favourite team starts losing. People don't change their political allegiance just because their party is voted out of office.

How often have you made a statement and then defended it when challenged? We equate consistency with substance – we like to be perceived as knowing who we are and what we want.

Not even the world's most powerful people are immune from this principle – the desire to remain consistent. Think back to the turn of the century when George W Bush, the American President who invaded Iraq due to the threat the country posed with its arsenal of weapons of mass destruction. After years of exhaustive searches, no weapons of this type were found. And yet, year on year, Bush referred to their presence. He felt it was more important to remain consistent than to be right.

Consider the Keysianesque response by the world's central bankers to the sluggish post Global Financial Crisis growth. Their response has consistently been to throw more money at the problem, with one major economy after another adopting highly stimulative fiscal and monetary policy. No-one's broken ranks. No-one's expressed the need to try something different. The urge to maintain a steady-as-she-goes we're-not-changing-now mindset dominates all thinking. The importance of remaining consistent – and maintaining a steadfast and predictable course – is considered crucial for the success of this experiment. The central bankers know how important this is to investors and the financial system as a whole. They understand this principle and the deeply held need we all have for the clarity and certainly born of consistency. Time will reveal whether the bankers were right or wrong. What we can appreciate now is why they are so completely wedded to their chosen course.

The German philosopher, Friedrich Nietzsche, observed that "many are stubborn in pursuit of the path they have chosen, few in pursuit of the goal".

Practical ways to use this principle

Look for an opportunity to get your prospective client to express what they are looking to achieve by working with a financial advisor.

In Chapter 4 I described a short narrative between an advisor and prospective client about whether their life cover was sufficient. Using SPIN we empowered our client to reflect on their position and conclude that they may not be as well-positioned as they initially thought. Your Need-payoff Question asked what action the client wished you to take. You can use the principle of consistency to maximise your influence in this situation by recording your client's response on a whiteboard or writing it down in your client notes. Later on in your conversation you can replay this commitment to your client: "I just want to be clear. Earlier we spoke about the need to review the amount of life cover you have. That there's a possibility that it is no longer sufficient now that you have taken out a mortgage and as you'll soon be the sole breadwinner. Is this still a priority?" Not only will the principle of consistency influence your client to answer "yes" to this question, I think you can appreciate how much psychological leverage you now have for your next meeting:

"I've done some investigating and some calculations on your existing insurance position. I think we both suspected that with a new mortgage and you being the sole breadwinner in a few months that it would be insufficient. I know from the last time we met how important this is to you to get right. Would you like to discuss how we can do this?"

When they start procrastinating over medicals or have second thoughts about the cost of the premiums, remind them why they chose that course of action. Here's some narrative for another scenario:

"Richard, remember what you said when we first discussed this? You said that if you were ever to suffer a heart attack or a major health setback, you wanted to get out of the rat-race and live your own life. Has this changed? Don't you feel the same way anymore?"

Most often people will impatiently nod their heads and say, "Of course I do. Let's get on with it!"

The advice process is often a lengthy ordeal for many people. Use words such as "you have told me many times how important [insert your client's goal] is to you. We need to take these steps to make it happen." If they start to lose momentum, remind them why they took the decision in the first place and challenge their consistency!

Enhancing the effectiveness of this principle

Here's an interesting insight that will enable you to import even more power into this principle. The commitment to remaining consistent is influenced by three factors:

- It is stronger when spoken rather than written. People are more strongly committed when they have expressed themselves with the spoken word. Get the person you seek to influence to tell you what they want from the relationship they have with you.
- It is stronger when said in the presence of another person. Get the person you seek to influence to meet you with their spouse or partner.
- And it is stronger when it is made voluntarily, not imposed. Allow the person you seek to influence to express themselves and find their way to their own decision. Any course of action that you impose will not provide you with any leverage should you need

to influence them at a later time. The most likely response will be: "Look, this was all your idea. Not mine. Now count me out."

Principle Three: Social Proof – people are strongly influenced by their peer group

Much of your instinctive thinking has taken millions of years to develop. Like many automated, hard-wired responses, there's a good reason for you to react in a prescribed way.

Your most powerful instinct is that of survival. When faced with grave danger we instinctively make "fight or flight" decisions. These situations seldom give you time to ponder and reflect over your next move. You receive a jolt of adrenalin and instinctively choose a course of action. But you are given a clue as to how to choose – you look around to see what everyone else is doing. The consensus – with its collective experience – is usually the correct choice and you follow the actions of the group. This instinct is the basis for the principle of social proof.

Look around and you'll see how powerful this principle is. It dictates what clothes we wear – the fashion industry is solely dependent on the principle of social proof. We wear clothes for warmth and protection. Why on earth should colour and style matter? It matters big time! Why? Because we have an enormous urge to fit in, to be perceived as stylish, classy, well-dressed, cool, and with-it!

One of the greatest statements that an anti-social individual can make is to wear clothes that don't conform to the norm. But in an example of just how powerful the principle is, even these non-conformers conform to a certain look, be it the gothic; carefree surfer; or couldn't give a damn, jeans with undies-exposed-at-the-top teenager.

The principle strongly influences the cars we buy. Main-street executives must drive this sort of car; rugged, do-it-yourself types that sort.

Why do smart entertainment venue operators make their customers queue outside? Wouldn't it be better to let people come in as they arrive and get them eating, drinking and dancing right away? Isn't that how you make money in that game? Not so. These people understand that anyone walking past an empty venue will continue walking. Their mind will suggest that nothing good is to be found here, if it were, there would be more people. Presto! Get a few of your mates to start a line and, before you know it, you'll have scantily clad youngsters happy to freeze in a queue for an hour just to get into your spot. They're thinking, "This place must be great. Look at all the people just waiting to get in!" Suckers.

My wife Leanne invited a representative from an educational company to come and demonstrate an exorbitantly expensive computer-based maths tutor for one of my daughters. I was curious to see what selling techniques would be employed to close this deal. I wasn't surprised to hear the principle of social proof applied. After failing to obtain the slightest sign of a buy signal from me during her hour-long demonstration, the rep turned to me and said "Mr Peer, many parents in your daughter's class appreciate the importance of good grades in maths and have gone ahead and purchased this program."

Key message to Dani Peer: if many of the other parents decided that this system was the best solution, who are you to go against the flow and decide otherwise?

The principle of social proof is an important determinant of the pricing on financial markets in the short term. This is what the legendary investor Benjamin Graham meant when he said "In the short run, the market is a voting machine but in the long run, it is a weighing machine." The daily, weekly and monthly pricing of assets on financial markets is dictated by sentiment, not fundamentals. Uncertainty is always present in financial markets, providing a fertile environment for this principle to exert significant influence. No-one really knows where markets are headed so participants are always looking for a lead. Guidance is provided by "experts" who belong to recognised institutions and are given prominence by the media. The herd follows their lead. Cialdini calls this particular situation "pluralistic ignorance",[19] a situation where no-one really knows what is going on and everyone looks to everyone else for direction.

A lot of the pricing on financial markets is simply relative. If share A trades on a price-earnings ratio of 15 and a similar company, share B, trades on a price-earnings ratio of 10, share B is said to be "undervalued". But few question whether share A is correctly valued.

There is simply a belief that the market is "correctly" valued – because everyone says it is (social proof). If markets were always correctly priced as the theory of Efficient Market Hypothesis suggests, why would there be crashes?

During my brief career as a fund manager I was part of this herd. It was only after a calamitous decline in share prices that I began to appreciate the importance (and danger) of pluralistic ignorance. In his book about market booms and busts, *Extraordinary Popular Delusions and the Madness of Crowds*, Charles Mackay opined that "Men, it has been said, think in herds; it will be seen that they go mad in herds, while they only recover their senses slowly, and one by one." Market sentiment is the mood of the crowd, not the aggregate of individual thinking.

Practical ways to use this principle

The principle of social proof is useful for moving the mind of our prospective client through both Stages 2 and 3.

Social proof and inclusive statements

In Stage 2 our client feels positively disposed towards us (rapport) and is prepared to accept (some of) what we say (trust). They still own their current position and will seek to defend it. We use the principle of social proof to loosen their commitment to their current position and to consider that what they now have is not optimal. We challenge their status quo by using "inclusive statements".

"Inclusive statements" is a term I've coined for a statement that suggests that others are doing what you should be doing. We make a suggestion to our prospective client that others have been in a situation similar to their own and have realised that this was no good and required action.

Let me provide a few examples that will clarify what I mean here:

- "I've got a dozen other clients in your position and each one of them has decided to switch their insurance premiums from stepped to level. They want to be confident – both now and in the future – that they'll be able to afford the protection they need."
- "More and more high net-worth people are setting up self-managed superannuation funds to give them the power to control where their money is invested."
- "Each of my high net-worth clients understands that a term deposit is just a parking place waiting for the right opportunity."
- "A lot of young people now realise the importance of insuring themselves. Not because someone depends on them financially, but because they don't want to become a burden on their family."
- "Most people that I've worked with in your position choose …"
- You're sitting in front of a complacent and disinterested accountant from whom you seek referrals. Don't launch into the merits of the relationship. Make use of an inclusive statement along the following lines: "I've obviously been having meetings with some other accountants who have practices similar to yours.

And each one of them seems to be concerned that unless they start to offer a broader range of services to their premium clients, these people are going to go elsewhere."

Social proof and testimonials

In Stage 3 our client is wondering whether it's worth the effort to do something about the problem they now accept they own (Stage 2) and if we're the right person to do business with. Testimonials can be very useful by encouraging your prospective client to think, "This person (who has given the testimonial) seems to be just like me. They're the same age and have a similar background. And they're facing the same challenges and concerns that I've got. If this advisor could help them then perhaps she's the right person for me. Let me hear what she's got to say." The key here is the ability of the person you seek to influence to relate to the person providing the testimonial.

Let's move to your next weapon of influence – the principle of liking.

Principle Four: Liking – People prefer to say 'yes' to someone they like
(and to those they believe like them)

This principle is partly based on our survival instinct – if someone likes me, then they're likely to have my interests at heart. It's also based on ego and the natural desire to be liked by others. Kids and especially teenagers will do almost anything to fit in with their peer group and are therefore very easily influenced by their mates. Adults feel the influential force of this principle too.

Sandy feet

A few years ago I was holidaying with my family in an apartment block right on the beach. There were big signs all over the place insisting that residents wash beach sand off their feet before getting into the lifts. Early in our stay, my mother-in-law failed to comply with this command. It was her bad luck that the aggressive chairman of the body corporate happened to get into the lift with her and read her the riot act. A distraught and teary in-law entered my apartment.

The chairman was a very successful businessman. He had a reputation for being tough and he was perfectly entitled to scold my mother-in-law. But there is the right way and the wrong way to do this and abusing and humiliating someone didn't seem right. It seemed that only an apology would clear the air for the rest of the holiday.

Demanding an apology from a guy like this would get me nowhere. So I applied the principle of liking. I walked up to the man on the beach and said something like: "You're a well-known and successful person. I'm someone who really admires your achievements. What on earth caused you to shout at a lady for something as silly as having sandy feet?" The guy looked very embarrassed. It wasn't what he did that I questioned. It was who he was. His reputation was at stake here. And he wanted it to remain intact. He wanted to be well thought of. He wanted to be liked. An apology soon followed.

What deliberate action can you take to be more liked?

You may be thinking that we've covered this ground somewhere earlier and you'd be spot on. We discussed in an earlier chapter how important our ability to build rapport is – and to make our clients feel at ease in our presence – in order to be perceived as trustworthy. I discussed what actions you could take to achieve this and your ability to listen with patience, respect and attentiveness will deliver great results. Listening, plus your ability to discover common ground with your prospective client, will get them thinking: "Not only is this advisor a decent, respectful person, but we seem to be cut from the same cloth. We both share a passion for sport and feel strongly about financial education." The journal *American Behavioural Scientist* explains this more quaintly when it says, "prospects are more willing to do business with an advisor akin to them".

There is one further tactic that Robert Cialdini shares with his reader that you may find useful, but only if very carefully employed. And that's seeking an opportunity to compliment your client on something they have achieved.

I met an advisor in Sydney who showered me with compliments about my tie. My very, very, average tie. I could see where he was going with this, but it was phony. He damaged his credibility. And he was less able to influence me. The key here is to offer genuine praise, not false flattery.

(Mind you, there is also some more interesting research that found men have a high regard for people who flatter them – even if untrue!)

Principle Five: Scarcity – People want more of what they cannot have
(and will value that which they have experienced difficulty obtaining)

You're hunting for a house. You walk into a property that you really like. The estate agent notices your interest and says something along the lines: "Yes it is nice. We're getting a lot of interest in this unit. In fact I'm expecting to get a signed offer later today." Suddenly your interest in the property doubles. You may lose it. You have competition. Someone else wants this beauty!

There is every chance that you have been manipulated. Estate agents often make use of the principle of scarcity to encourage buyers to submit an offer. They've got another classic that you've probably been subject to and that's the one-liner, "God isn't making land anymore". This can mean one of two things to a buyer: If you don't buy your bit of earth – and sooner than later – you're going to miss out, or buying land is a good investment because there's a natural supply constraint (God).

Movie houses and particularly live theatre make common use of this principle. How often have you seen in newspapers and billboards "Only 7 days left to see this epic production." And, curiously, these warnings seem to run for weeks and weeks. Retailers are shameless with phony deadlines when running sales. My local mattress store has been having a closing down sale for years.

My old stockbroker was an enthusiastic disciple of this principle. He'd recommend a share, and just to spike my interest would add after the recommendation – "but you can't get them".

"What do you mean I can't get them?" I'd ask, with interest.

"They're hen's teeth." He would reply. "They're never offered."

"Well I expect you to get me some." I'd demand, with urgency.

Any student of the market knows that in most cases sellers appear all over the place as soon as a bid is raised. You can get any share, so long as you're prepared to pay for it.

Let's go back a few decades to when I was young and single and reflect on my mostly unsuccessful attempts to attract the opposite sex. I regularly followed Paul McCartney's advice when he sang "It's a fool who plays it cool" on the legendary single *Hey Jude*. Yep, as soon as teenage infatuation set in (usually after about five minutes of stilted conversation) I started describing my desire for a long-term relationship. Flowers and perhaps champagne were part of the second date and more often than not there was no third. I accumulated quite a repertoire of break-up lines: "I like you as a friend", "I think that you have a great personality", "I'm not ready for a long-term relationship", and many more.

Like most young people who think that they have all the answers, I just simply kept plugging away with the same tactics. I even regarded more successful suitors with some contempt. They were fast and loose whereas I was dependable and committed. I simply couldn't understand that the more disdain they showed, the more desirable they seemed to become.

Of course, with hindsight it all makes perfect sense. *People want more of – and place a greater value on – that which they cannot have or experience difficulty getting.* This is the principle of scarcity.

You may be thinking that scarcity isn't an issue in the world of a financial advisor. That there are lots of advisors for clients to choose from and almost every product we sell has an almost infinite supply. That's not the case. But before I share some ideas about how you can make effective use of this principle, let's explore where it could best be used.

I believe that the principle of scarcity is best employed to move a client's mind through Stage 3, and can also be effective in the crucial Stage 5. Let's focus on Stage 3 first. During this stage your client is wondering whether it's worth the effort to proceed. They've moved past Stage 2 and realise that their current position is suboptimal. But they're considering procrastinating. They are also wondering – should they choose to take action – whether you're the right person to work with. So we have two hurdles in Stage 3 – motivating action and positioning yourself as the best person to take action with.

Using scarcity to motivate action – time in the market

There's a great Chinese proverb that says: "The best time to plant a tree is twenty years ago. The second best time is now." Most prospective clients that you meet with will be under-saved. This could be due to procrastination and a lack of discipline, or poor budgeting and an under-allocation to building wealth. Whatever the reason, most people miss out on the opportunity to get *time in the market* to do the heavy lifting of wealth creation. People these days are looking for the silver bullet. They risk their savings with aggressive gearing to make up for lost time. They demand high returns without appreciating the possible downside this thinking has. Your approach is to discuss the importance of time in the market. That, until now, they have not seized – have in fact lost – the benefit of the vital contribution that time makes to a person's wealth. You suggest that while taking action years ago would have been the best choice, taking action today is a close second. That the time available for all of us to create wealth is scarce and that every moment should be grasped with a sense of urgency. A sound decision today may avoid the high-risk journey of tomorrow that many who continue to procrastinate are forced to take.

Using scarcity to motivate action – you won't be in mint condition forever

Most people believe that they'll take out insurance when they're good and ready, certainly not until a clear-cut need arises. You would have come across such bullet-proof and headstrong individuals on your travels. You apply the principle of scarcity to this situation by suggesting that personal insurance is not a right. It is in fact a privilege that is available to people who meet the health, occupation and lifestyle requirements of those who take on the risk of insuring them. You continue to explain that should the time come when your client seeks to take out cover, that even if the insurer is prepared to accept their risk, it will be increasingly difficult to get that cover at standard rates – the lowest rates available. If your client believes themself to be fit and healthy, and that in fact turns out to be the case after various health checks, then now, today, is the only time that they can be absolutely certain that they will get both the protection sought and at the best rates available.

Using scarcity to position yourself as the right advisor to work with

Some financial advisors are not only unaware of the principle of scarcity, but in fact decrease their ability to influence by becoming more available to the clients they seek to influence. These advisors are prepared to go out of their way at ridiculous hours of the early morning or night to fit in with clients. What they communicate in this situation is: "I'm available whenever you want me." Contrast this with some medical professionals, when you feel only too lucky to get an appointment within a month.

Consider the following scenario. You've just had an hour-long meeting with a new prospective client. You have received no signals at all that this person wishes to proceed with you, yet they would be a perfect fit for your services and you're very keen for them to become a client. You're worried about losing control of this tenuous relationship by asking the person whether they would like to proceed. You don't want to hear the words "I'll think about it and get back to you." My suggestion? Turn the tables on them. Instead of chasing, take a step back with the words: "It was lovely meeting with you, Paul. Let's both take some time to reflect on this meeting. I will call you in a couple of days and we can consider where to take it from there ..."

Rodney is one of the toughest advisors I know. He strongly believes in the value of financial advice and this shows in the high conviction he brings to his conversations with clients and the respect he has for both his profession and himself. When he senses a lack of conviction in a prospective client he almost shuts up shop. He'll say something like: "Look, I sense that you are not committed to the course of action that we've just discussed. I'm not going to take this further until I'm convinced otherwise. I have other people seeking my services and I want to work with people who value what I do. I'm happy to meet again if you take a different approach to how we can work together." Is this aggressive? Absolutely. Does every prospective client return? Not a chance. But many do. This is a blunt but effective use of the principle of scarcity.

I remember attending a Million Dollar Roundtable function at which an advisor explained that he always made appointments for the following week. "I can't meet with you this week. Can I suggest 10 a.m. next Thursday?" There's a practice in Queensland that specialises in providing an immaculate service to selected high-net-worth individuals. They make very effective use of the principle of scarcity in two ways: they won't meet you unless you have been referred by an existing client, and you have to wait at least a week for an appointment.

When I suggest to advisors that they make themselves less available, I get some strange looks. But just as an over-amorous suitor is soon dismissed, a client feels no urgency with an easily available advisor. McCartney's advice is no good for relationships and it's not good for our business. You'd be a fool not to play it cool.

Principle Six: Authority (Credibility) – people defer to experts

As with the principle of liking, I discussed the importance of credibility in an earlier chapter when considering the factors that define trust and how trustworthy we are perceived to be. I described several factors that contribute to our credibility that included our qualifications, experience, formal recognition of our achievements, how we dress, where our offices are located, the words and language we use and even where we admit ignorance.

Because I introduced credibility in the context of trust and not influence, I'd like to make a few more observations about this principle and how you can make good use of it.

People defer to experts. In fact, adults will go to almost any lengths on the command of an authority.

Again, we are hardwired in this way for the benefit of society. The ability of authority to exert influence is the basis of government. Influence through authority is required to maintain law and order. Influence through authority is necessary for delegation to take place. Thus most state and corporate structures embrace the principle of authority to influence.

The principle of authority is so powerful that it even works when it shouldn't. Let me explain. Many personalities command authority because they are well known. They may be sports starts, pop stars, wealthy business people, politicians and actors. We tend to assign them credibility because of their high profile, not their skills or expertise. Advertisers make use of this hardwiring to associate person and product. Witness how many personalities recommend a particular product, the merits of which they are totally unqualified to give an opinion. What does George Clooney really know about coffee? I can recall adverts where Ian Thorpe has been used to recommend a breakfast cereal and Steve Waugh a supplier of investment products. We don't sit back and muse whether Thorpe's credentials are any better than ours with regards to cereals, or Waugh's in the case of investment solutions. Had Thorpe endorsed a particular energy booster, or Waugh cricket gear (or even suntan lotion!) the link would have been more credible. Due to the prowess of the principle we have no need for the link or logical flow.

We instinctively, subconsciously assess the credibility of another person before allowing ourselves to respond to their requests or their suggestions. As a society we need to know who to trust, who to follow, and who to ignore.

If an acquaintance warned you about travelling to a particular country about which you judged they had little knowledge, you would most likely choose to ignore them. If your travel agent gave you the same warning, you would take this more seriously. After all, they should know what they're talking about. But if the *government* posted a travel warning you would probably cancel your trip. Each bit of information came from a source with increasing amounts of credibility.

A drunken reveller at a noisy pub shouting "fire" would be laughed at. A fireman in uniform would be instantly obeyed.

One of this decade's most influential books on selling is Matthew Dixon's *The Challenger Sale*. Although this book is concerned with the business-to-business (B2B) sale, we find in it an important insight into the principle of authority and its application in a business-to-customer (B2C) experience typical of the advisor-client conversation. Dixon describes several sales profiles: relationship builders, problem solvers, hard workers, lone wolves and challengers. Dixon explains that "challengers" use their understanding of their prospective client's situation to push that client's thinking and are not afraid to share even potentially controversial views. The reason challengers can make use of this particularly effective sales style is because they are perceived to be an authority in their chosen field. Unlike the relationship builder who relies on rapport, the problem solver who solves whatever the customer thinks their current problem is at the time, the hard worker who puts in the hours or the hyper-confident lone wolf who relies on their unique style and personality; the challenger uses their authority born of credibility. They reign supreme in B2B land because they know better than their customer what's good for them.

It seems to me that some advisors forget that they have a natural authority that is a product of their credibility, so they choose to adopt a profile other than that of the challenger. I absolutely appreciate that the architecture of the B2C experience is different. But I firmly maintain that if we believe that we are indeed professionals, that we are experts in our chosen field of providing financial advice, that this demeanour, this conviction, will translate into authority in the eyes of our clients and will, in turn, provide us with a greater ability to influence. On the other hand, if we allow ourselves to be governed by sales targets and activity metrics and see ourselves more as distributors of product, we may struggle to employ this particular weapon of influence.

Authority (Credibility) is the last of the six Cialdini Principles I introduced at the start of this chapter. There are two further principles from other texts that have great value and broad application in our circumstances – the principles of fear and sequencing.

Principle Seven: Fear – fear is uncomfortable and therefore motivates action

Fear is a powerful emotion. It's uncomfortable, unpleasant and therefore motivates a person to take action to find relief. It's very difficult to influence a complacent individual to take a desired course of action. Fear shatters this complacency. It is a superb motivator to guide your client's mind through the hurdles in Stage 2 of our cognitive map. Stage 2 has got your client thinking "I'm okay. I know what's good for me. I've got this far without a financial advisor haven't I? I've got a point of view – I also read the papers. I've already got a trusted advisor – my accountant looks after me and has so for years. I've already got a plan." If you are not able to shake this complacency you have very little chance of progressing the conversation. Keith Eades in his book *The Solution-Centric Organisation* puts it neatly when he says, "Clients don't value solutions to problems they don't think they have." I'll tweak that a bit and say that clients aren't even interested in hearing about solutions to problems that aren't hurting them. David Lapin, in his magnificent book on leadership, *Lead by Greatness*, nails it when he says, "It is a tragedy of the human condition that discomfort is the most effective propeller of meaningful change." The principle of fear is one of the most potent weapons of influence you possess.

How can you use fear to influence another person? It may sound obvious, but by simply helping the person you wish to influence to find it!

Most of us will have had an experience whereby we're cruising along with life and somebody says something that rattles us. You're watching a sports match with a few mates. One of them casually remarks, "Jeez, I'm pleased I pulled my cash out of that property fund. I hear it's about to go under." You happen to have a sizeable investment in the same fund. You get goose bumps. Your chest tightens. You'll either start interrogating your mate to find out everything he knows, or you'll count the minutes to take the first gap to speak to someone who can help you.

Fear creates action.

In June 1997 I was thrilled with the birth of my first child, Jessie. And I started to worry (it's amazing how vulnerable you become as a parent). Crime in South Africa had started to gain some real momentum – it wasn't just some guy who was hijacked, it was now your cousin, your neighbour, your colleague.

I remembered that dreadful day when I was told that one of my staff had been shot in a shopping centre parking lot. He had been taken to hospital in a helicopter and was in a critical condition. I remembered another of my staff who arrived at the office looking like he hadn't finished getting dressed. His cuffs were open and sticking out of his jacket and he wasn't wearing shoes. He had just been mugged.

I started to fear. That distant thought of immigrating became front of my mind. My priorities changed. I was motivated to take all sorts of action. I didn't even wait for the Australian High Commission to post me the required visa documentation. I got into my car and drove to Pretoria – a city an hour away from Johannesburg – to collect them.

Fear provokes action.

But the old-style approaches to creating fear in prospective clients no longer work. Years ago life insurance salespeople were trained to ask questions like…

"So what keeps you awake at night?", or

"What would you do if your business partner was killed on the way to work?" And the classic:

"How would your family cope if you weren't around tomorrow?"

We need to be more subtle. The professional advisor helps their client to discover fear by joining the dots. We assist those we seek to influence to appreciate the consequences of their actions – or in most cases lack of action.

Let me clarify this approach with a detailed example and then a few more at a higher level…

The client who's wedded to property

Property ownership has created more wealth for Australians than any other asset class. And it has done so in a consistent, non-volatile manner. There are also generous tax breaks and the thrill of driving past your own bricks and mortar. Shares, on the other hand, create angst with their constant repricing and the scars of the GFC are still relatively fresh. And there's little yield for those who bunker down in cash accounts. Convincing a client to limit their property exposure and diversify sensibly often requires some firm persuasion and the principle of fear is your weapon of choice.

Your client's mind is in Stage 2. "I'm okay. I have three investment units. I'll sell one, pay off the mortgage of the other two and that's all I need for a comfy retirement."

You gently enquire about what assumptions they have made with regards to capital growth. This is important for their plan to work as they have no chance of paying off the three mortgages (nor do they plan to). The way they see it, all that is required is reasonable appreciation (no more than the historical average) in order to sell one property and pay off the mortgages of the other two. "Look – I've done all the numbers on a spreadsheet."

You ask what would happen if the property market flattened out or even lost value. Your client replies that they consider this "very unlikely". Both you and your prospective client know that if the market trend breaks they may retire with three units worth less than what they paid and three mortgages that have still a significant amount owing on each of them.

You then throw two doubts on the table. You mention that Australia is the only first world country not to experience a severe property collapse in recent times. That much stronger and richer countries like Japan, the United States, Britain and almost all of Europe have suffered substantial falls in property prices. You're not saying it will happen in Australia, you're just suggesting that being too convinced, too stubborn about our beliefs can have consequences. You then mention that property prices, like everything else, are determined by supply and demand. For prices to move up demand must remain strong. And the main determinant of demand is affordability. If you cannot pay for something you cannot demand it. While interest rates are at generation lows (courtesy of the GFC fallout) credit is very affordable and therefore demand is strong. If interest rates move up (and here you can decide whether to digress and discuss the concept of reversion to the mean if you reckon your client's up to it), affordability, demand and thus prices can be expected to move down. You then remain silent while your client digests this and again enquire whether a more diversified approach should be explored.

I've walked you though this conversation to demonstrate what I mean by "joining the dots". This world is just too complicated for most people to understand the potential consequences of their chosen course of action. That's the beauty of working with a financial advisor – it's a golden opportunity for a client to test their thinking and assumptions.

Here are a few more "dot joiner" opportunities for you to help your client find the fear needed to galvanise them into taking constructive action:

Clients who are apathetic about retirement planning and intend to rely on an Aged Pension

You could discuss that many countries, Australia included, don't have any fund from which pensions are paid. That current pensions are paid from current tax receipts, and borrowings where these receipts are insufficient. You'll make mention that two major problems have started to emerge: the debt of the countries that have been doing this has become such a burden so as to threaten their financial future (you may refer to Greece here and make mention of the deeply worrisome US Federal Debt and their ongoing need to lift their debt ceiling); and the demographic bulge of baby boomers in and entering retirement and the excruciating pressure this puts on the state's ability to meet pension obligations. For really rigid mindsets you could provide a brief understanding of why one of the world's largest car manufacturers, General Motors, nearly collapsed during the GFC and could only be saved by sharply cutting back on pension entitlements – not only to those approaching retirement, but to those in retirement! You conclude by saying that this is a rarely understood risk that we financial advisors call "statutory risk". The risk that the rules behind our assumptions will be rewritten.

Again, you remain silent while your client digests this and enquire whether they would like to work with you on a retirement plan that will reduce their reliance on what the state will or won't provide.

Client who are apathetic about structuring their life cover

Help them to understand that where the proceeds of a policy are paid to a single beneficiary, all income earned on this lump sum payment will be taxed in the hands of that beneficiary. That by creating a testamentary trust on death, income may be able to be split and any tax liability considerably reduced.

Young clients who are apathetic about taking out any form of personal cover

Explain that you fully appreciate that they are young and free and have the world at their feet. You understand that they have absolutely no commitments and are not surprised that insurance has not been at the top of their mind. What you would like them to consider is a scenario where they do not meet a tragic end at a young age, but are left alive after a serious accident or illness and require substantial care and medication for many years. Would this be a tremendous burden on ageing parents? Would state healthcare suffice where a private solution would at least make a disaster more tolerable?

A few comments before moving onto the next principle…

The principle of fear, when used by the professional financial advisor with a great degree of integrity, is not crass manipulation of the uninformed. It's helping people appreciate the possible consequences of their decisions by applying logic and facts that assist them to join the dots, to close the loop, to understand the downside where they have only seen the upside.

One of the greatest benefits of working with a financial advisor is the opportunity for a client to gain perspective. To more fully understand their current position and the potential outcomes of adopting and maintaining that position. The salesperson always supports their customer, responds to what their customer says and wants. The professional advisor guides and challenges their clients. We don't so much sell as help the people who seek our guidance to decide what's best for them and then to choose whether to work with us to achieve that outcome.

Principle Eight: Psychological Sequencing (Anchor Points) – people rely on whatever information they have when making a decision in conditions of uncertainty

The road traffic in Vietnam's big cities is unbelievable. It's in a perpetual state of motion. Like blood, it flows all the time, slowing and speeding up to accommodate new entrants, those changing lanes and those exiting to join another pulsing black vein. Pedestrians wishing to cross a street time their entry and move with practised calm in front of oncoming vehicles that slow imperceptibly to create a moment's gap. The preferred transport is the motorbike and scooter. All seem to be continuously hooting, not so much to warn but to make aware.

I spent a week there courtesy of a large institution that had organised a "study tour" to reward and enhance relationships with the company's most successful and committed supporters (principle of reciprocation alert!). We'd just arrived in Hanoi and a group of us decided to take a walk after the long flight and get a feel for this exotic city.

We were soon spotted and surrounded by several "cyclo" drivers touting for our business. A cyclo is a three-wheeled bicycle with a shaded cushioned seat in the front. It looks like a combination of bicycle and wheelbarrow. The hirer sits in luxury while the driver pedals furiously from behind. It's a great way to see the city up close and we were all keen to take a ride.

A big, beefy Queensland advisor appointed himself as our negotiator. The opening offer from a wizened driver, who seemed to speak the best English, came in at the equivalent of 100 Australian dollars. This sounded a reasonable fare to me for an hour of someone's time – especially when they were expected to pedal for that full hour. Our man rolled his eyes, gave us a "leave this to me look" and countered with fifty. The old driver looked pained and shook his head. "Seventy-five" (or whatever the Dong equivalent was), he said. "Sixty and no more." Our guy was playing tough. "Okay" came the old guy's resigned reply. Knowing a good deal when we saw one, we hired five cyclos, a stack of Dong notes changed hands, and we had an eye-popping ride around the old part of the city.

On our return to the hotel we wandered into an informal briefing from our tour operator. She shared a few local words which I still remembered years later when I visited Vietnam again with my family. At the end she gave some guidance about where best to shop and what we should expect to pay. Her last words were, "And I highly recommend that you hire a cyclo and go on a street tour. You should expect to pay about ten dollars for an hour's ride." The Queensland advisor turned bright red.

A few days later I used this incident in a presentation on the psychology of persuasion. It was a perfect example of one of the principles I wished to discuss. "How was it," I asked, "that we were happy to believe that we were on the receiving end of a bargain when we were in fact paying six times more than the going rate?"

Psychological sequencing, sometimes referred to as anchor points, is a deceptively simple weapon of influence. The principle is that people make judgement calls against the first piece of information they hear. We use whatever information we have as an "anchor" against which to judge whatever new information we receive.

Retailers used this principle all the time when stock goes on sale. Adverts will read: "Was $80 now only $40." It's so important to state the original price – that sets the anchor point. Unless you know the original price, being told that a particular item only costs $40 is meaningless. But once you are informed that an item that sold recently for $80, now only costs $40, you are strongly influenced to buy. Percentage discounts work the same way. The original price is your anchor.

My friend Ryan owns a car service and repair business. My car was in his repair shop because I had failed to twist my head 180 degrees and had not spotted an immovable wooden electricity pole while I was reversing.

The damage was not major but I was left with an ugly dent on the rear of my car. I mentioned to Ryan that if the repair was expensive that I would learn to live with the dent. He, of course, was keen to get the business. So he cheerfully broke the news that my rear door, bumper and various panels would have to be replaced at a breathtaking cost of $5,000. I thanked him and asked for my keys. And he smiled and said he was pulling my leg. For $1,200 he could get the car back to mint condition.

After the number $5,000 this seemed like a bargain. But when you think about it, $1,200 is steep for a minor bump! Had he quoted this figure up front I may have easily declined.

I worked with Robert Redenbach, a very accomplished professional speaker, a few years ago. Rob was a self-defence expert and had provided his services to several highly-respected law-enforcement agencies. He wrote a short book about his tactics called *Be Your Own Bodyguard.*

Soon after the book was published he received an invitation to speak at a function. His material had piqued someone's interest. The caller asked his fee for an hour-long keynote. Rob was totally unprepared for this question and said "eight". The first number that came into his mind. Eight hundred dollars for an hour's work seemed ludicrous and he immediately regretted his off-the-cuff response.

Like almost all consumers, the caller felt the need to test the price and to see if he could negotiate it down a bit. "Eight thousand? I feel that a fee for this sort of work should be in the region of around $5,000. Would you be prepared to do it for say $6,000?" It took ten strong men to lift Rob off the floor.

Anchor points are a great way to create and manage expectations. And the principle doesn't only work where numbers are involved ...

My family went on holiday to Fiji with a few other families. We arrived just after New Year's Day. About ten minutes after we unpacked the wind became fierce and it started pouring. This went on for the first eight days of our stay. Even though the remaining four were lovely, we all felt badly let down by the weather. On returning to Melbourne a mate with a lot more local knowledge than I remarked, "Fiji in January? That's the middle of their cyclone season. You're lucky you saw the sun at all." If I was armed with that expectation as my anchor point I would have been prepared for the foul weather and celebrated when the sun came out. On second thought, I probably wouldn't have gone at that time of the year in the first place!

Here are some practical ways to apply this principle

- When discussing your fees with a client. You may suggest that your premium service is priced at $5,000 per annum. However, you do have a standard service that you feel would be most appropriate in the client's circumstances that would only cost $3,000.

- Few people really know how much they should pay for insurance. Say you present a quote for $2,500 per annum, this may appear cheap or expensive – depending on your client's anchor point. If you make mention in early discussions with your client that full cover is usually in the region of 3 to 7% of a person's income (or whatever you consider to be a fair and appropriate benchmark), they will have already formed an expectation of the cost. So if your client's actual income is $70,000, $2,500 equates to just under 4%. You therefore present the cost as being "at the lower end".

- For an impatient client: "This first appointment usually takes about an hour and a half. But as you are in a hurry I reckon that we can cover the ground in an hour, tops."

- To make the completion of a lengthy application form seem easy: "You've probably heard that insurance documentation can take the whole morning to complete! Don't worry. This shouldn't take us more than thirty minutes."

- To prepare a client for the medical underwriting process you could tease that the life office usually insists on piles of forms and several health tests. "But for you, we just need a blood test."

- To get two referrals a month from your best referral sources who might view this as a big ask: "Look, ideally I'd love to get around five referrals a month from you. Let's initially aim for two and we can build it up from there."

Final word

A weapon in the wrong hands can cause much harm. When using these principles of influence we need to consider the question: when does *influence* stop and *manipulation* begin? Do you remember the days when cigarettes where advertised on TV and at the movies? Not the disturbing adverts that warn you against smoking (principle of fear), but the adverts that showed beautiful people diving off an expensive yacht into a calm, sapphire sea, or skiing down a picturesque slope with an idyllic mountain range in the background. The adverts suggested to us that these people were winners in every way – fit, beautiful and rich. And what did they do as soon as they'd climbed back onto the yacht and dried off; or completed their downhill slalom and removed their skis? Why, they'd light up a smoke! I grew up with the Lexington cigarette slogan, "After action satisfaction". The application of the principle of social proof is clear: the rich and famous smoke, if you want to be like them, so should you. The intent here is obvious: British American Tobacco didn't give a hoot about giving you tips on how to become one of the jet set, they were only concerned with cigarette sales – pure manipulation. These adverts were so effective that they are now banned. President Nelson Mandela, on the other hand, was concerned with reconciliation. He made full use of the principle of liking. Not to manipulate – he certainly wasn't looking for conservative-minded rugby supporters to vote for him. He used a weapon of influence to reconcile, to unite, to harmonise. Not to promote throat and lung cancer.

Should the emerging profession of financial advice make use of these weapons of influence, then? Absolutely. But we need to be very clear when we do that we are using them to influence and not to manipulate. It all boils down to intent. If our primary objective when employing these principles is to hit a sales target set by our employer, or a certain level of profitability if we are self-employed, then we are most likely manipulating our prospective client. If our main purpose is to provide advice that aligns with the needs of our client, then we are influencing our prospective client.

Key points from this chapter

- The psychology of persuasion is a mainstream branch of psychology. It provides those who master its principles with powerful leverage to motivate others to take action.
- We discussed the theory and practical application of eight principles:
  - Reciprocation: people have a natural urge to respond to a kind deed
  - Consistency: people have an inbuilt desire to be consistent
  - Social proof: people are strongly influenced by their peer group
  - Liking: people prefer to say yes to someone they like and to those they believe, like them
  - Scarcity: people want more of what they cannot have and will value things that they have experienced difficulty obtaining
  - Authority (Credibility) – people defer to experts
  - Fear: fear is uncomfortable, unpleasant and therefore motivates action to find relief
  - Psychological sequencing (anchor points): people are prone to rely on whatever information they have when making a decision in conditions of uncertainty
- Weapons of influence don't require a licence to use. However, they do require a professional to be clear and aware of the difference between manipulation and influence.

Chapter 6:

The power of storytelling

"Think of story as a mnemonic device for complex ideas."

Annette Simmons
Author, Speaker, Storyteller

I was very excited. This looked like the kind of investment that ticked all the boxes – a very simple asset with a generous yield. When my family arrived in Australia we were stunned by the price of everything. One of the most stunning prices was the cost of parking a car in Melbourne's CBD. I kept thinking *what a terrific investment a parking lot would be*! It would have all the advantages of property (remember, God is not making land anymore) but without all the aggravation of ongoing maintenance and needy tenants. I could just imagine a flat piece of ground and a spritely pensioner looking to earn a few extra dollars collecting the required fee from exiting motorists. So when my financial advisor introduced me to just such an opportunity, I was thrilled.

It was even better than I'd imagined – this wasn't some bumpy piece of dirt on the outskirts of Melbourne's business precinct. This was a parking lot slap bang in the heart of Sydney; underneath the famed Opera House, to be exact. The numbers looked great and the business model was easy to understand. This was just what I was looking for. The asset was in the form of a property trust and I went in big. What could go wrong with investing in a parking lot?

Quite a bit, I discovered.

The first few years went swimmingly. The returns were as advertised and I congratulated myself on the quality of my network that had enabled me to seize opportunities like this. I even visited the car park like a proud landlord would gaze fondly on their building. I marvelled at the rates visitors were prepared to pay and thrilled in the knowledge that this was my revenue.

Then things started to cool. The first salvo whistled over my prized investment in the form of much higher parking levies as a cash-strapped Sydney City Council lashed out in all directions. This wasn't an inflation increase. This was a giant impost. A letter from the trust's manager informed me that this was a small set back and that returns would dip slightly, but that there was nothing to be concerned about. Enter the financial deep-freeze of the Global Financial Crisis and asset prices went into free fall (bullet-proof car parks as well).

The next letter from the trust's manager told me that all distributions were now suspended, a demand of the bank which part-financed the purchase. I was told that, due to the fall in the value of the asset, the loan-to-value ratio was no longer acceptable.

At the same time another problem emerged. The car park at the Sydney Opera House isn't any old piece of bitumen with a few white lines – it's a fairly complex property with air conditioning, fire management equipment and numerous mechanical exits. It turns out that the old manager (the trust's management had changed hands mid-GFC) never really took much interest in the infrastructure itself. They weren't property types, being much more comfortable with spreadsheets and glossy product documents. The new team undertook a complete review and found that substantial maintenance was required. (You can see that this isn't going to have a happy ending.) The drop in the asset's value plus the costs of getting the car park into an acceptable condition meant that the investor equity had been well and truly destroyed. This was the information I received in the last letter from the trust manager. The final paragraph informed investors that the trust had been handed over to administrators. I had, not for the first time, taken a very big financial step backwards.

Stories

There's no better way to deliver content than through a story. The content can be dry and laced with numerous facts. The content can be complex and difficult to grasp. But put it in a story and people become engaged. They listen. They enjoy the experience. They understand your message. They join the dots. They remember.

Every professional speaker you will have heard knows this. Almost every major event on a financial advisor's professional development calendar provides an opportunity to hear great ideas from accomplished people packaged in engaging stories. I remember feeling absolute awe for the accomplishments of Dr William Tan. Dr Tan suffered from polio as a child and is confined to a wheelchair. Not only has he carved a career as a paediatric surgeon, but he has competed in – and completed – marathons on every continent. His story of losing his equipment prior to competing in an Arctic marathon, and the toil and physical agony he endured to complete that event, totally reset the expectations of those of us in his audience. In theory, we all knew we could achieve much, much more in our lives. However, that knowledge had little traction. Package it in a story, and wow!

I still remember the energy and excitement of the men from *Afterburners* – ex F18 pilots who packaged their messages of "Flawless Execution" in stories. After several weeks on the road I became good mates with Phil and Westy. Both had been instructors at Canberra's elite fighter pilot training school. Phil had seen action in the second Gulf War. They challenged their audience of financial advisors to consider their practices in the same way they viewed their cockpits. They spoke about colleagues who had "died with a smile on their face" – pilots who had no idea that they were about to crash and lose their lives – and about how those who fail to plan both in business and in life could suffer shocking outcomes.

I learned from the stories of Rob Redenbach that there was no substitute for experience. That your value to yourself and others comes from using and refining what you know. Rob was an ex-infantryman and an ex-bouncer. He developed his own unique self-defence fighting style. He refined this and perfected it in the toughest pubs in Australia. Confident that he had something of substance, he offered his solution to the most respected units in the world working with Britain's SAS and the FBI in the United States. He regarded his greatest achievement as being invited to become head of training for Nelson Mandela's personal protection unit.

I spent a few weeks on the road with Ron Barr, founder of Youth Insearch, an organisation that supports young people who have lost trust in our community and who have slipped to the sides of society. The organisation I worked with at the time wanted Ron to share his stories with financial advisors for a very good reason: many of the youth that needed his support started their journeys to hell because a financial calamity hit the family – most often in the death or permanent disability of a breadwinner. He explained the profound consequences where a lack of planning and bad luck intersect. How ordinary, comfortable lives can be shattered, homes repossessed and friendships ended as a result of enforced moves. How easy it is for this to happen to anyone who has not adequately protected themselves through a minimum of proactive thinking.

His stories were punctuated with interviews from some of the kids on his programs. While many in his audience wept, everyone was reminded of the role they played as financial advisors in making sure that this did not happen under their watch.

All these people have accomplished so much, and there is so much that we can learn from them. Just like your clients have so much to learn from you. How they choose to communicate their wisdom is crucial to how much we are able to take away. They don't burden us with facts. They don't kill us with PowerPoint. They thrill us with stories and through this, move us to think and to take action.

Why do stories work?

Simply put, people love to hear stories. Psychologists believe that this is due to us associating stories with our early childhood. The joy of our parents reading a bedtime story or the relief we felt when our teacher put arithmetic aside in favour of a compelling tale. Stories engage our imagination. They transport us from our reality into limitless possibility. Stories allow us to relax, to go with the flow and to enjoy the experience.

Stages 1 to 3 of our cognitive map are the key hurdles to getting our prospective client to seek our services. In Stage 1 we are challenged by our client's defensive mindset – they fear that we are going to make them do something that won't be in their best interests. In Stage 2 we are challenged by our client's apathy, inertia and resistance to change. In Stage 2 our client is prepared to believe that, while we are not a threat, there is nothing much for us to do. A suitable story, well delivered, can be just the catalyst that encourages our client's mind to vault these two cerebral hurdles. Stories can be equally useful in moving our client's mind through Stage 3 (is it worth the effort? Can this person sitting in front of me really help?).

Stories can help you build rapport, thereby reducing polarity and creating trust. Stories can be the ammunition used in weapons of influence, used to help your client find their fear, used as an anchor point, used to show what others in similar circumstances are doing, and thus employ the principle of social proof. Stories can be used to help your clients discover financial goals they'd never considered before. And stories can be used to illustrate the importance of investor behaviour management and the discipline of diversification, for example, not going overweight Sydney car parks just because you think it's an absolute winner.

Anecdote is an organisation that trains business leaders to tell stories. They explain that when we speak to someone with the intention of getting them to do something, we *push* our conversation. But when we tell a story, we involve the listener and they *pull* meaning from our story. "Stories engage people as a participant in the communication. Stories deliver facts in context with emotion and therefore inspire people to take action."[20]

Stage 1 requires us to remove polarity and create trust. A story is the ideal medium. You cannot tell people that you are credible. You cannot tell people what you value. They need to find this in you, usually by the words you choose. A story that explains why you have chosen the profession of financial advice, what beliefs you embrace strongly, your journey as an advisor, your successes and, yes, your failures, is powerful ointment for the rough and scratchy start to any new relationship.

Stage 2 of our cognitive map explains that people embrace their position – their thoughts, beliefs and viewpoints – whether good or bad. We are all hardwired to suffer from something that psychologists call *confirmation bias*. It makes us difficult to help and shocking as investors. Confirmation bias is what it says – we are always on the lookout to confirm what we think is correct. Notice next time you begin to read an article, the contents of which you vehemently disagree with. Note how you skim through the writing and even stop reading after the first couple of paragraphs. You mutter quietly to yourself, "This idiot doesn't know what he's talking about." You spot a heading that aligns with your view and thoroughly enjoy the read, feeling really good that your position is supported by others. Your client experiences a similar emotion if you challenge their thinking in Stage 2. Here your tactic is not to challenge, but to help your client discover why what they have embraced is not the optimal position. A story is the ideal way for a client to self-discover. You tell the story; they come to make up their mind.

Gary Klein is a psychologist and decision-making specialist. He believes that stories are the ideal medium "for making sense of complex situations and as a conduit for meaning and decision-making".[21]

Finding your stories

Anecdote talks about three buckets:

Your stories: Every one of us has got a story. No, we have many. What made you choose your profession? What memorable moments have you had with your clients? Most financial advisors, other than those who have just set up shop, have clients who have suffered tragic accidents, severe illnesses or who've died young. Too few employ these experiences in compelling narratives. This is not unprofessional. It is not ghoulish. It is life and all those apathetic, she'll-be-right souls out there should know this and, in that way, be motivated to become more proactive. Think about your successes and brightest moments, but also your failures and disappointments. What were your most profound learning moments?

Other people's stories: Financial advice is a people's business. We speak with hundreds of people each year. Which of their stories have left you moved? Thinking differently? Have motivated you to take action?

Books, movies, current events: A newspaper has a hundred stories. Some movies share a powerful lesson. There's so much material out there.

Enhancing your stories

There is a lot of literature that supports the enhancement of stories. I can understand the merit of investing time and effort to engineer a story for a keynote presentation and for business development events. I'm not convinced that there's merit in a financial advisor fine-tuning a portfolio of stories to deliver depending on the direction that conversations with clients may take. I would simply suggest that you identify a handful of stories that will assist in moving your client's mind through Stages 1 and 2 – and then use them in practice to see how it feels, what impact you create and what adjustments you need to make.

If there are a few broad pointers to a "better" story, they are:

- Ensure that your story has purpose. Consider what you want to achieve by telling the story. Is it to break the ice and get a prospective client to feel more comfortable with you? Is it to communicate something personal so that your client has a better understanding of your purpose, your values and your closely-held beliefs to help them develop trust in you? Is it to introduce discomfort with your client's status quo and to motivate them to discover why their position is not as sound as they'd like to believe it is?

- Keep it short. Anyone who has ever worked with me will laugh at this point as I tend to be a bit long-winded with my explanations and stories. I recognise that this is not a strength, and have worked on being more concise.

- Keep it simple. Avoid lots of characters, numbers and events. Stories are there to simplify your message. There no time in a business meeting for a Charles Dickens plot.

- Make it personal. Make it about you – your feelings, your clients, your experience. You need not have been involved in the actual event that you describe. But how you personally relate to the event is where all the value in the story lies.
- Make it about people, not things. We all want to hear about the triumphs and tragedies of people we can relate to, not things like financial markets and planning strategies. Where confidentiality is not an issue, share names and personal details.
- Similar to the above point, weave some emotion into your story. *Anecdote* put it well when they say, "We remember what we feel and, despite their painful sounding name, we don't tend to remember bullet points."[22]
- Ensure that your listener is able to relate to the characters in your story. They should be able to visualise themselves in a similar scenario. They should feel as though you were almost talking about them.

I'll end this chapter with an intensely personal story which I have told many times and which still gives me goose bumps every time I do. Although the circumstances during which this story took place were very different, its message endures: *be very careful what advice you give people who trust you and are likely to follow through on what you say…*

South Africa in the late 90's was an unsettled place. Politically it seemed to be working, but socially it was a mess with dysfunctional education and health services, road mayhem and crime was out of control. Those who were able to emigrate, but who had decided to stay and to see what the New South Africa offered, started to dust off their papers and plan a life in a new country.

I'd been invited to a meeting of so-called young and influential Jewish businesspeople. The purpose of this meeting was to recognise the influence we had in our community and to call on us to instil optimism in those who we came into contact with. It seemed a reasonable request. There were many positive aspects. South Africa's Black majority had been enfranchised and a new middle class was blooming. The country had been welcomed into the family of nations and international entertainers and sports stars were becoming a regular attraction after decades of isolation. Many new business opportunities had presented themselves and many people started becoming very wealthy. But behind closed doors we worried. Terribly. Those with money used whatever means they could to get around the country's strict exchange control regulations to set up nest eggs in other lands. Many families quietly secured visas that would enable them to live in safer places. The country and many of its people where somewhat bipolar – thrilled with a sports victory one day, terrified on hearing about a friend experiencing criminal violence the next. We were used to this dichotomy and reasonably relaxed about being asked to promote the cup-half-full perspective. But everything changed when a man got up and made his way to the lectern.

We all knew who he was – a high-profile and very well-respected tax barrister. He acknowledged the purpose of the meeting and, while agreeing with the sentiment, asked for a few minutes to share a story with us. After that, he said, we were free to make up our minds and to do whatever our consciences dictated.

He told us about an American lawyer sent to Germany in late 1945 to prosecute those charged with war crimes. The lawyer was selected because he was fluent in German, having lived in Berlin prior to emigrating to the United States just before the war. He left because he was Jewish and Hitler's Germany was not a place for any Jew who could leave. The lawyer soon found himself questioning a gaunt and shattered concentration camp survivor. The survivor was giving evidence against some of the camp's guards. The lawyer found himself distracted. He thought that he recognised his witness but just couldn't place him. When the court recessed the lawyer approached the survivor and asked if they had met before. To which the survivor replied:

"Yes we have met before. In fact I was your neighbour in Berlin. Remember? The guy with the big clothes factory? We use to talk every now and then across our fence. I often asked you what you thought of Adolf Hitler and his plans for Germany. You were a well-connected person in a big law firm. You always told me that things would work out well. That Hitler was all bark but was doing good things for the country. I listened to you, a fellow Jew. I invested more and more in my business. When it became obvious that things were not going to work out the way you had suggested I could not leave. Everything I owned was in Berlin. You, on the other hand, had developed connections and secured visas and arranged for your family to leave Germany. I listened to you and now I am a survivor. Now I have nothing. I have lost my wife and my children and everyone else I loved. They have all been murdered by the people you now prosecute."

There was absolute silence in the room. The tax barrister stepped down. The organisers – to their credit – didn't bother to try to get the meeting back onto their agenda. People huddled in small groups, deeply moved by what they had heard. I left feeling very troubled.

I have always been a very positive person. I instinctively see the doughnut rather than the hole. My friends always joked that I'd be the guy who would "switch off the lights" – would be the last person to leave. Until the birth of my first child, that was probably true. But somehow in my need to remain positive I had become deceptive. While screaming myself hoarse for the local sports teams, I had also secured my Australian visa. When others sought my counsel I communicated my commitment to South Africa and shared my optimism for the country's future. I said to myself that I wasn't in the business of making others worry. I saw myself as a source of confidence and stability. This powerful story was a bucket of cold water tipped over me. It was a hard slap in my face for not respecting the need for candour, for the truth when big decisions are made based on what is said. From that day I have been absolutely committed – when there is anything of substance on the table – to never giving advice that I would not be totally comfortable following myself or watching someone I love adopt.

Final word

"Maybe stories are just data with a soul."

Brené Brown, Scholar, Author, Public Speaker

"Sometimes reality is too complex. Stories give it form."

Jean Luc Godard, Film Director, Screenwriter, Film Critic

"Storytelling is the most powerful way to put ideas into the world today."

Robert McKee, Creative Writing Instructor

"The human species thinks in metaphors and learns through stories."

Mary Catherine Bateson, Writer and Cultural Anthropologist

Key points from this chapter

- People love to hear stories. They engage our imagination, explore limitless possibilities and allow us to relax.
- Stories can help us progress our client's mind through each step of the cognitive map. They are particularly useful for the hurdles we confront in Stages 1 and 2. Stories enable us to reduce the resistance and polarity found in Stage 1 and to overcome the complacency and inertia associated with Stage 2.
- The company *Anecdote* explains that while a normal conversation is pushed onto the listener, a listener pulls meaning from a story.
- You can find your stories in three places: your own experiences, those of others and from books, movies and current events.
- Don't over-engineer a story. It should not sound practised.
- For a story to have the desired impact it should contain some of the following qualities: Purpose, brevity, simplicity, personal not general, about people not things, some emotion, and relatable characters.

Chapter 7:

Why you?
Articulating
your value

Irwin squinted at me over the dinner table. We'd probably both had a bit more to drink than we should have. We'd been crossing swords for over an hour, each of us holding, sometimes slightly and sometimes markedly, different opinions of how the world at large was playing its cards. The hot conversation turned super nova when we moved to money, markets and Irwin's financial advisor. Shares had been running well, but, in Irwin's opinion, his portfolio was underperforming. Looking like he'd bitten a lemon, he spat out, "My advisor is an idiot. He can't make me money." When I said, "Irwin, that's not his job", his expression was a mix of confusion and derision. "What do you mean that's not his job? That's what I pay him for!" No you don't. There's more to it…

We expect our doctor to make us healthy. We expect our accountant to save us tax. We expect our lawyer to draft a good contract. We expect the pilot to fly us safely, the architect to produce a set of plans, the computer expert to remove the virus that stuffed up our laptop. But what is expected of a financial advisor? That depends on who you ask. And this represents a major challenge for our emerging profession and how we sell our services.

Where we don't add value – slaying some sacred cows

Many current and would-be clients believe that our value lies in delivering two outcomes: we are expected to shop around to find the cheapest insurance premiums and we are expected to manage money to deliver superior investment returns. Perhaps saving tax is a distant third. The professional financial advisor understands that the value we deliver has little to do with either cheap premiums or superior returns.

What "cheap" really means

The professional financial advisor understands that premiums may appear cheap because they are on a stepped rather than level basis, or because the policy terms are extremely onerous or contain broad exclusions, or because the insurer has priced his product aggressively to capture market share and this will have to be repriced in the near future as optimistic actuarial assumptions don't pan out and margins become commercially unacceptable; or for any number of other reasons. We understand the insurance industry is extremely competitive and the cheap premium of today is the average or even dear premium of tomorrow.

Why we can't sell "outperformance"

It is extremely tempting to offer a market exactly what it wants. There are many people who see wealth creation as a competition. The highest return wins. They seek to beat the market, to outperform a benchmark, to receive a "great" return (whatever this may be in the eyes of a particular person). You can call them investors, traders, speculators, whatever you wish. You cannot call them a client, or even a prospective client. The professional advisor knows that "outperformance is neither a financial goal nor a financial plan".[23] Outperformance depends on your client's anchor point. It is relative to their perception of what financial markets have offered and it is relative to how their mate's portfolio has performed. People who chase outperformance don't make it because there is no purpose and no end goal. Nick Murray, one of our profession's leading thinkers, expresses this wonderfully when he says:

"A portfolio is not a plan, and the neurotic quest for 'outperformance' is very often an attempt on the investor's part to avoid the pain of planning: the necessity to set goals, to figure out what those goals will cost, and to make the commitment to save – to defer gratification – enough to fund those goals, assuming reasonable rates of return over time."[24]

We can't offer our market outperformance. Not only because we cannot deliver on this promise (I discuss this more in the next few paragraphs) but *because it's not what our clients need*. We will educate our clients to understand that the performance of their portfolios must be measured not against financial markets, not against that of their mates', but against their own plan.

We are not investment experts but strategic experts. Any financial advisor who is able to consistently deliver risk-adjusted portfolio outperformance is in the wrong profession. This person should be in the funds management game with all its inherent leverage. Investment experts should not waste their time managing hundreds of individual relationships, rather their focus should be on running their own top-quartile fund. We understand that portfolio management is best outsourced to a specialist who has the expertise and resources required to invest the wealth of others. We understand that even in expert hands wealth can be destroyed. That experts can get it wrong, sometimes horribly so.

We cannot consistently time the market nor can we consistently select the best investments

There are many people who believe that the financial markets can be timed. That an expert – such as a financial advisor – knows when it is time to buy and when it is time to sell, and that when the timing is right to buy, that the best investments are able to be identified. It is easy to understand why so many hold this perception. The media loves to provide a simple explanation for every market move that suggests anyone involved in investing with their eye on the ball could have profited, if they'd been half alert. There are numerous investment advice sites on the internet that will inform you just what to buy and when. *Surely*, thinks our client, *my advisor can keep half an eye on Bloomberg's and take action when necessary? Somehow, thinks our client, my financial advisor has access to uncirculated analysts' reports that enables him to spot the gems in the mud.*

I mentioned my relationship to Arthur Andersen early in this book and how the company met its demise due to the collapse of Enron. But did you know that ten out of the fifteen share analysts who followed Enron were still rating the stock as a "buy" or a "strong buy" as late as 8 November 2001, which was three weeks after the initial report of the company's hidden losses appeared in *The Wall Street Journal* and about two weeks after the US Securities and Exchange Commission announced an investigation of Enron? Analysts provided our very own Westpoint with an "investment grade" rating. You may recall the array of stars accorded to the funds of Basis Capital. And Timbercorp debt came "highly recommended" by a local online outfit.

When asked why his organisation was heavily geared in all the wrong investments just as the Global Financial Crisis struck, the then CEO of Citigroup, Chuck Prince, famously said: "As long as the music is playing, you've got to get up and dance." Almost every senior manager, economist and analyst at all the major Wall Street investment banks didn't see the GFC coming. Almost all of these firms would have collapsed if they were not taken over by other institutions with massive assistance from the Federal Reserve Bank.

This is why Nick Murray says a value proposition based on the suggestion that we can somehow select, time and therefore outperform "is a lie"[25] and that we cannot sustain a business on a lie. All we can do is "rent money"[26] until our client "figures (us) out".[27] The result is constant client departures and the constant need to attract new clients. Murray ominously warns, our practice will become a "referral free practice".[28]

The late Stephen Covey gave us a similar warning through his concept of "circles of control". Covey describes three concentric circles. The one in the centre he labels "control", the next, "influence" and the outer circle "no control". Covey explains that in some narrow, focussed way we do have control over a limited number of variables in our lives (and those of our clients). As the environment in which we operate expands, we may only be able to exert influence and at best encourage a desired outcome. The outer circle is the largest circle thus suggesting that we have no control over the majority of activity that takes place around us. We can control what we wear on a cold day. We can influence our colleagues to adjust the office thermostat so that we feel more comfortable. We have absolutely no control over the weather.

A professional can add value, and charge a fee, where they have control or influence over an outcome. However, the professional should never suggest that he is able to provide an outcome over which he has no control.

Our tax loopholes are quickly disappearing

Finally, we understand that, as the Western welfare state's need and appetite for tax receipts grows each year, the opportunities for us to deliver ongoing value in the form of tax planning diminish. Loopholes are being closed all the time and much of the value we delivered in the past, particularly at the end of each financial year, has been reduced. We are left to ensure that retirement contributions are maximised and whatever few deductions are available utilised.

The professional financial advisor understands this, her market does not. Their misconceptions ensure that we start almost every conversation we have with a prospective client by having to unpick unhelpful perceptions around what they think we do and replace these by what we actually do that will be of value to them.

Value and the cognitive map

Stage 2 of the cognitive map requires that we gently challenge misconceptions, primarily about our prospective client's existing position. Stage 3 requires that we provide some high-level thinking about how the concerns and weaknesses uncovered in Stage 2 could be addressed (to motivate action) and that we present a compelling case why we would be the most appropriate person to address these issues. And Stage 4 requires that we expand on the broad representations delivered in Stage 3. How we articulate and present the value we bring to the relationship, and the depth of our belief and conviction in what we say, will play a major role in our ability to guide our client's thinking through these stages.

The eureka moment, the mind-opening epiphany that characterises all of the most successful financial advisors who regard themselves as working within a profession, is the recognition, the absolute certainty, that their work is not to chase down the cheapest premium nor to deliver the highest return. It is an awareness that their value is much greater than this, and an ability to communicate that value whenever they engage with someone who is seeking their services for the first time. In this chapter I will share with you the most wonderful and powerful ways of viewing our profession. We will rise above premiums and returns and consider where the real value lies in the advisor-client relationship.

A few words about value

Value truly lies in the eyes of the beholder. It is not an absolute concept. Value often remains dormant and then suddenly rears into existence, into awareness, when a catalyst is applied. In most cases that catalyst will be the words you choose to unlock your client's awareness about where the value in a relationship with you can be found.

Stephen Kozicki is an accomplished author and presenter. He often relates a personal experience to illustrate just how subjective value can be …

Steve was enjoying a barbie with a group of friends one lazy summer afternoon. You can picture the scene –

men standing around the barbie swigging beer and wine, swapping war stories. Wives and partners fixing the salads, some helping their kids, others sitting down chatting. The wine runs out and Steve scurries inside to get another bottle. Standing forgotten on his desk is a red he'd been given earlier in the week by a particularly satisfied client. He pops the cork in the kitchen, walks outside and starts to top up the closest empty glass. His mate says a casual cheers and then stops and shouts, "Hey, hey! What's going on? Are we celebrating something today?" Everyone turns around and looks at Steve. He stands there a bit bewildered. "What do you mean?" he asks. To which his friend replies, "That's a $600 bottle of wine you've just opened. It's a Penfolds Grange." Steve didn't know that. Being the guy that he is, he probably would have thought that a great day in the sun with close friends was just the right occasion to open such a bottle. To him, it was just another bottle of red. To his mates, it was liquid gold.

How often do we read about someone buying a masterpiece or a rare stamp at a garage sale? Closer to home, how often have you offered a premium single malt to a visitor only to have them dilute it with water?

For something to be considered valuable, we must *recognise its value*. Too many of us only recognise this value when we lose it. In the words of rock and roll legend Ral Donner, "You don't know what you've got until you lose it."

The value of financial advice is nowhere near as clear cut as a Penfolds Grange or a newly-discovered van

Gogh. Our challenge as a profession is to come to some consensus as to where we believe the value of financial advice truly lies. If it's not the cheapest premium or top-quartile returns, *then what do we do that is of value and for which we should be able to levy a fee*?

The consequence of not answering this question is profound. Our work will be defined by a market that is ignorant of both its needs and the solutions it should be seeking. If we adopt the retail mindset – the customer is always right – and simply respond to the requests of those who seek our services, we will do many people a great injustice. We are not order-takers. We are not target-chasing salespeople. The professional is burdened with the responsibility of determining and then advising their client not on what they *want*, but on what they *need*. This awareness presents us with much higher hurdles. It's easy to sell a kid a lolly. Not so easy to educate him on how to floss his teeth. That's why enabling skills are so crucial for the professional financial advisor. We are no longer concerned with the easy sale – we are committed to the right outcome. It is up to us to link what our client needs to what we can offer and, in that way, assist her to find value in the advice relationship.

Before we investigate where our true value lies and how we can articulate this – and in this way inspire our market with a much bigger vision of the value of working with us – there is one small detour to be taken. And that is for you to explore your own mindset.

Finding your "why"

I said earlier that value lies in the eyes of the beholder. Your client will view value from their perspective and you will view value from yours. How you respond to the rest of this chapter depends on how you see your purpose as a financial advisor. Value and purpose have a strong link. *If what I do aligns strongly with my purpose, then I will believe that what I do has value.* If you are not clear on your purpose, the reason why you have chosen to practise as a financial advisor, then the concept of value is more marketing text than a source of personal power.

I introduced Simon Sinek and his philosophy in Chapter 1. Sinek's whole message is centred on one word – *Why*. Sinek believes that the answer to that one-word question is not only the source of your personal power (that feeds qualities such as conviction and persistence), but crucial for your ability to influence and inspire others. Finding your *why* gives meaning to what you do. When you find your purpose you are unstoppable. People want to jump on your train, become part of your journey, bask in your certainty.

People and organisations that are crystal clear on their *why* considerably outperform peer groups and benchmarks. It's also the reason why people choose to do business with you. Sinek says, "people don't buy what you do. They buy why you do it."[29] Value communicated without an underlying conviction always sounds fake. The words "this is important" ring hollow when said in a dull monotone.

I'm reminded of a conversation I had, soon after finishing university, with a friend of my late father. Pieter phoned me out of the blue to introduce me to a new business venture. "It's called Herbalife", he said. I was still wet behind the ears and had no idea what multilevel marketing was all about and had never heard of Herbalife. Pieter laboriously explained the model, stopping every now and then to catch his breath (he was a heavy smoker). His monologue went on for ten minutes but I dutifully remained attentive. Towards the end of the call he started to fade but rallied himself for the finale he expected would secure my buy-in. "Dani", he whispered weakly, "it's not just the money you'll make. What's best of all, you get to use all their products. And I can honestly say (quick few shallow breaths for desperately needed oxygen), that I have never felt better since I started using them." Punch line! It was crystal clear to even a young, naive and untrained ear that either this bloke had no conviction in his product, or he was delusional. I suspect the former. He had simply read from a script supplied by the franchisor. No conviction. No belief. I saw no value and didn't give this opportunity a moment's further thought.

What's your *why*? Have you discovered it? Are you looking? Why do you get up before the sun? Fight the traffic? Seek to influence and motivate lethargic people? Stress out at every market dip? Fight underwriters, diligently complete professional development assignments, keep up to speed with every software upgrade?

I'd like to share my *why* with you. Why am I such a fervent, rabid, dedicated, devoted supporter of our profession and the value we contribute to our clients? I hope that this may inspire you to start or to continue the search for your own (unless you have found yours too).

My *why*, and perhaps all *whys*, tend to be a product of a set of beliefs.

I believe that money is important to most people. Not because money can buy happiness, but because it buys choices. A lack of money invariably means hardship.

I believe we have entered a period of world history where a set of coincident factors have contrived to make the accumulation of sufficient funds – and thus the ability to achieve financial goals – incredibly difficult without professional guidance, the type provided by financial advisors.

I believe a significant part of the increase in the value of assets (both financial and property) has been on the back of a multi-decade growth of credit. This credit boom introduced two forms of inflation into the system – one obvious and one very deceptive.

The obvious inflation was in the form of consumer inflation. But this was muted due to significant productivity gains, particularly in high-cost items such as motor vehicles and household durables like electronics and white goods. Consumer inflation has also been dampened by the authorities reworking the actual basis by which inflation is calculated. Substitution for lower cost items and the recognition of technology improvements are all fed into a black box to produce lower and lower inflation numbers. Volatile costs such as food and energy are excluded from some measures. The upshot is more and more financial stress in an era supposedly characterised by low consumer inflation.

We have also experienced a far more substantial inflation but this has deceptively been re-labelled as "wealth creation". I refer here to the increase in asset values. The credit boom has elevated asset values in two ways. The first is somewhat obvious – easy credit juiced by low interest rates and minimal deposits have delivered a property boom. The second impact that credit growth has had on asset prices has received little recognition. It should be appreciated that a dollar borrowed today is no-one's expense but someone's revenue. If I borrow an additional $10,000 each year, which is not reflected as an expense in anyone's P&L because no-one paid this to me in return for my labour, and then I spend this money on goods and services, this $10,000 is simply profit to the overall economy. *Credit artificially inflates macro profitability* which, in turn, has been the leading driver behind the performance of equity markets.

Both property and equity values depend on robust credit growth. Central banks know this and have done their damndest to ensure that credit growth does not stop – even to the point of eliminating the cost of borrowing and penalising banks for not lending. I believe that this journey is not sustainable. Unless credit is invested in assets that can produce sufficient income to both service and repay the debt – which has not been the case – eventually this game must come to an end. I believe credit growth and inflation are now peaking and that the easy ride this gave to asset pricing will end.

I believe developed world demographics, specifically an ageing population, will bring considerable stress to retirement funding. Current unfunded liabilities now measure tens of trillions of dollars. Combine the demographics with the substantial advances in healthcare that translate into increasing longevity and the already alarming forecasts will probably turn out to be woefully understated.

I believe globalisation and labour arbitrage will continue to put substantial pressure on the cost base of developed countries, thus suppressing the rate of increase in major P&L line items such as salaries, wages, other employee benefits and rent. This, in turn, will lower consumer demand, economic growth and the profitability of those corporations who rely on the domestic markets of these countries.

I believe we are stuck in an era of big government that not only absorbs considerable resources from the economy, but is characterised by increasing interference in the private sector, thus raising the costs and complexity of doing business, driving down profitability and impacting asset values.

I may be wrong in some or all of my beliefs. But these are my beliefs and they explain why I have found such purpose – my *why* – in the financial planning profession. I don't believe that "she'll be right". I don't believe that the state will have the resources to continue to rescue underfunded citizens. I don't believe that gearing up on a few investment properties provides any chance of a financially-secure future. I don't believe in a silver bullet.

I do believe that the world has reached an important inflection point, and that securing the services of a good financial advisor is no longer optional. Our profession has come of age and provides a service that can and will make an important difference.

You may hold totally different beliefs from mine. That's fine. My challenge to you is to discover what you believe in and how this translates into *why* you do *what* you do. While your value lies in *what* you do and *how* you do it, your *why* is your fuel. Your *why* gives a sense of purpose, a sense of meaning to your career. And that *why*, and the passion with which you communicate it, will inspire those who seek to do business with you to sit back and listen to the immense value that only you can provide.

Where do we create value?

Let's now turn our attention to where our true value lies and how we can articulate this. I'll introduce you to four perspectives from leading thinkers in our field and finish with my own narrative, which is a composite of my research and the inspired thinking of some of the great advisors I've worked with. The objective here is to provide you with ideas about how you can find your purpose and express your value with both power and deep conviction. To boldly and confidently reply when asked by anyone – friend, family, prospective client, or just the curious – "What is it exactly that you do? Why would someone want to work with you?"

Dan Sullivan's perspective – leadership, relationship and creativity

To Dan Sullivan, founder of *Strategic Coach*, who we met in an earlier chapter (remember the DOS Conversation?), the value offered by financial advisors is not found in the advice process. It's not found in the completion of a fact find, the development of an SOA or the implementation of a strategy. That is a commodity that can be offered by anyone. (In fact, more and more online solutions are doing just that.) Sullivan believes that "the entrepreneurs who are truly thriving in this environment are doing so by creating unique value for their clients … that is doing something that clearly differentiates you from your competition and at the same time protects the price you can charge for your service."[30]

Sullivan identifies three components of value creation: Leadership, Relationship and Creativity.

Leadership

We live in a confusing, complex and somewhat intimidating world. We are told as youngsters that the world is our oyster. All we need is a good education and a strong work ethic and the doors of opportunity will swing open. We soon learn that this is not the case. We learn that most important decisions are not easy to make. That, even in a nanny state designed for consumer protection, we face dangers that must be avoided or addressed, that there are predators who don't have our best interests at heart. We are also exposed to many tempting and constructive opportunities. But how do we evaluate these? How do we decide which to seize and which to let pass us by? The more choices we have, the more decisions we are expected to make, the more paralysed by indecision we become. We prefer to ignore the dangers of inadequate insurance and underfunded retirement portfolios. We prefer to ignore the opportunities presented by creative minds and global access. We become closed to new possibilities and remain stuck with a particular viewpoint – often to our detriment.

The financial advisor provides leadership. The financial advisor provides direction. Sullivan tells us, "Value is created when we help others gain a sense of simplicity in their thinking about the future."[31]

Relationship

Few people flourish in life without the support of others. It could be a family, a coach, a team, fans and followers, a massive organisation. We operate at a higher level when we are supported, encouraged and held accountable. "Relationship is about providing confidence."[32] Of course there are the do-it-yourselfers. But most people seek a trusted relationship – especially when faced with decisions that concern substantial issues. Can someone buy insurance online? Or through a call centre? Sure. Most people seek the wisdom, guidance and counsel of someone they trust.

The financial advisor is the ideal person to provide this wisdom, guidance and trust. To be the client's counsel. "Someone who is focusing on their strengths and playing on their team."[33]

Creativity

We are bound by what we know. And most people know very little about financial planning. This is not a criticism. We live in the age of specialisation. Hundreds of years ago we all had to be somewhat skilled at hunting, cooking, sewing, fighting, farming, first aid and many other capabilities. Now our economy works through millions of specialists providing their skills at different times in the production of goods and services.

The financial advisor is able to provide options, alternative ways of achieving the outcomes our clients seek. We know that our advice contains many assumptions and many trade-offs, that our profession is as much art as it is science. We understand that value lies not in the process of financial advice but in the options, ideas, alternatives and paths we can offer our clients so that they may choose the journey that resonates the strongest with them. Our experience and knowledge of the environment through which our client journeys enables us to be creative. It cannot be replaced by a formula, a fixed process or an algorithm.

According to Sullivan, the financial advisor's value has nothing to do with product or technical advice. He doesn't mention investment returns or product price. Instead, Sullivan argues that our value has everything to do with providing our clients with direction, giving them support, and creatively suggesting solutions to help them reach their financial goals.

George Kinder's perspective – finding our client's why

George Kinder is the father of the *Financial Life Planning* movement. Like Sullivan, Kinder believes that the value in the client-advisor relationship does not lie on the technical level, but within a philosophical, psychological and spiritual framework. Kinder strongly believes that our primary role, our value, is to help people find purpose, a *why* that powers their journey. How? Like Sullivan's DOS (described in Chapter 4), Kinder offers us a structured conversation – EVOKE:

E: Exploration. Here we build rapport and trust by having a completely client-centric conversation. We ask questions that gently compel our prospective client to consider their circumstances and attitudes. Not so much about their financial position, but how they got there. What are her beliefs about money? What positive and negative life experiences have influenced his mindset?

V: Vision. Here we explore possibilities and desired outcomes. Our aim is to inspire, to get our client to consider outcomes they had not had the courage or motivation to explore, prior to meeting with a financial advisor. It's just like the "O" (opportunity) in Sullivan's DOS questions.

O: Obstacles. We now consider what could prevent the goals and desired outcomes from manifesting. Again, not unlike Sullivan's "D" (danger).

K: Knowledge. This part of the conversation revolves around the tactics and strategies that should be employed to seize the goals that emerged when Vision was discussed and to avoid or mitigate the dangers identified when Obstacles were considered.

E: Execution. The conversation ends with a review of how the strategy will be executed. What action is required? What transactions are involved?

Both Sullivan's DOS and Kinder's EVOKE elevate financial advice from a technical wealth creation (and protection) experience to that of discovering one's purpose. They set up a much more ambitious (and valuable) journey for both client and advisor.

When reflecting on your wealthy clients, consider this exceptionally insightful quote from Larry Arnn, President of Hillsdale College, a liberal arts institution based in Michigan: "The world is full of rich people who are miserable. And the world is full of rich people who are not. And the difference is not that they have money. The difference is the ones who are not miserable have some idea of something worthy to do with their money."[34]

These clients are not so concerned about whether they can afford private schooling for their kids or a comfortable retirement. Instead, they need a trusted resource who has a deep understanding about both them and their resources and who can open their minds to possibilities as yet undiscovered. Our role is to help these clients operate at the highest level of Maslow's

Hierarchy of Needs – the level of Self-Actualisation. Helping our clients find deeper meaning that translates into fresh goals that, in turn, translates into fresh financial plans.

Bill Bachrach's perspective – values

While Sullivan and Kinder offer us a framework for a conversation of substance, Bachrach focuses on the secret ingredient to both DOS and EVOKE – *values*. In a nutshell, this suave, slim San Diego-based thinker, trainer and keynote speaker suggests that our greatest value lies in helping our clients find their value. He calls this "value clarification". Bachrach believes that "most financial advisors limit their conversations and planning to get the funds and sell the insurance"[35] and has developed the philosophy of "Values-Based Financial Planning™".

The bedrock of Values-Based Financial Planning™ is the "Values Conversation". From my perspective, Bachrach differs subtly from Sullivan and Kinder in that his emphasis is not on goals but on values. His guidance is for the financial advisor to initially concentrate on what is important to the client, not the client's goals and aspirations. *That we seek to identify values and then define goals.*

I strongly resonate with Bachrach's philosophy. I believe that wealthy people have "potential". Their money gives them options. It has latent power. The challenge for the wealthy is how to convert this potential into something that has meaning for them.

The professional financial advisor is the best-placed person to fulfil this need – the need to discover what is most important to them (their values) and how this can be expressed in a practical way. The deepest value lies primarily in ongoing discovery; the planning (and most certainly the implementation or execution) is mostly technical and generic.

Values-Based Financial Planning™ is about asking questions of a prospective client that no one else has and, in that way, helping them discover something important about themselves. Stage 2 of our cognitive map requires us to unsettle our client by helping them discover that their status quo is sub-par. With many clients this will be through the discovery that they are underfunded or underinsured or, most likely, both. This is a problem that must be fixed. With wealthier clients the value we deliver is not so much that they have problems, *but that they are missing opportunities*. We can take these people on an inspirational high road rather than operating within the tight constraints that characterise our work with clients where we tend to optimise several trade-offs.

Nick Murray's perspective – behaviour management

Nick Murray offers a narrower but substantial contribution as to how our profession delivers value. He comes at us from two directions. Murray doesn't believe our value comes from selling outperformance or timing the market, and his work featured heavily in the discussion on where financial advisors *don't* provide value earlier in this chapter. Instead, he presents us with a substitute that is not only of greater value to our clients, but that has integrity, is able to be consistently delivered and will reduce and even eliminate the angst felt by every advisor when markets tumble. Murray offers us a promise we can make, can deliver and one that addresses the core needs of our clients.

An epiphany

The epiphany that Murray helps us discover is the fact that "people underperform their own investments".[36] Let me clarify this point. At the time of writing, the ten-year return for the S&P 500 index is around 7.7% per annum. The actual number is not important. What is crucial is to realise that the majority of retail investors (the typical advisor's client) who invested in this index would have received a return considerably lower than 7.7%. This is not an assumption but the result of substantial research conducted by organisations such as Dalbar Incorporated and Lipper Incorporated. The principle that Murray uses for his value proposition – and which is supported by these two organisations – is that the performance of a portfolio has very little to do with the actual outcome a client receives and that a *client's behaviour has a far greater impact*. It is absolutely correct that a client who invested their savings in the S&P 500 index ten years ago would have received a return of 7.7% per annum. *But only if they had remained invested for the full ten years and very few clients would have remained invested for the full ten years.* Most would have panicked and sold out at some point in that ten-year journey. Many would have bought back in. Some may have sold and bought several times. Many people would have sold at or near the bottom of the market: that's what causes a market to stop falling and to make a base – all the weak hands are out. And ask yourself, when would many have bought? Well after a recovery had started to clearly present itself, when it felt safe to move from cash into growth assets again. In the same way that we are genetically hardwired to respond in a particular way when a weapon of influence is applied to us, so *we are genetically hardwired to make a total hash of managing our investments*. The fight or flight impulse is all too powerful. We see our retirement nest egg battered to half its value. We see a life of cat food and cold nights ahead. And we panic. We flick the switch. It's only human. The converse is also too true. We hear stories from our mates and colleagues about the riches they are making and again panic that we are being left behind.

Murray gives us a substantial and enduring basis for a value proposition on a platter: "Behaviour is the dominant determinant of real life returns."[37] Our role is to maximise client outcomes, not portfolio outcomes. This requires behaviour management. Not portfolio management. This is a consistent value proposition. This is what we should be offering as advisors.

A value proposition of substance

We capture this value proposition in three words: Faith, Patience and Discipline. We discuss our value proposition whenever our client asks, but certainly when we believe their mind rests in Stage 3, when they are asking themselves "why this advisor? What is she offering that others are not? Does what she says make sense? Do I think she can deliver? Does this sound difficult to do?" We will provide further details when we sense their mind has moved to Stage 4. We can then go into more depth about behavioural finance, the findings of Dalbar and Lipper and even relate personal experiences of clients who ride the waves of inevitable market volatility (sure, you've been woken up at night. Sure, all your best clients will get your mobile number) and who continue to experience success because they receive the support and guidance needed from someone they trust. (You'll get this too if you choose to work with me.)

Faith

You cannot be a good investor if you fear the future. At any time there are numerous reasons why investing money in volatile assets can end in tears. The advisor brings perspective and history to the relationship. The path of history is up. Things get better. Great companies prosper. You play the role of money psychologist acknowledging your client's fear (and, in some cases, greed), helping them to understand why they are feeling that way, talking them away from the edge of the cliff and saving them from the wealth-destroying mistakes that others who lack the necessary support and counsel are making.

Patience

Creating wealth should be as exciting as watching paint dry. It's something that should be happening in the background while our client gets on with his life.

Unfortunately the system is rigged against our success. Streaming data (just watch how often the market addict reaches for their smart phone – I know, I'm one), 24/7 financial channels, experts of all sorts appearing everywhere with insights that promise to make a fortune, ensure that money – and where it's invested and how it's performing – remains top of mind. Our clients are being fed messages all the time suggesting that they're missing a trend, that they're in the wrong investment, and that there are better opportunities. The value offered by the financial advisor lies in our ability to instil in our clients some constructive beliefs. That the best approach is to buy and own a portfolio of high quality assets and to *leave it intact over the course of our plan* (give or take a bit of rebalancing). That's what Warren Buffet means when he says, "our favourite holding period is forever".

Richard Thaler and Shlomo Benartzi are among the world's leading thinkers in the field of behavioural finance. They determined that the more often we look at our portfolio, the lower the returns we will receive. This is because the more often we do so, the more likely we are to ditch something that appears to be lagging and to go chasing something that is currently shooting the lights out (or will soon shoot the lights out because it comes with a good story).

We earn our keep by instilling a quality largely absent from the modern world – patience.

Discipline

Discipline ensures we remain committed to the financial plan. We will bring discipline to our client relationships by insisting that an appropriate asset allocation (an asset allocation as required by the financial plan) be adopted and not allow our client to bias their portfolio to their particular taste. We'll insist on being diversified even when our client is convinced that going overweight in a particular opportunity will bring them great riches. And we'll ensure that our client's portfolio is rebalanced by trimming winners and buying laggards, even as our client screams for their winners to be left to run and demands that their losers be jettisoned – the same natural tendency we all have to buy high and sell low and thereby bringing ruin to our financial fortune.

"We know that a goal-focused, planning-driven portfolio – steered by the stars of faith, patience and discipline; properly asset allocated, broadly diversified and regularly rebalanced – is the investors' only hope of achieving superior, long-term, real-life returns."[38]

Sullivan, Kinder, Bachrach and Murray all emphasise the value of the relationship between the professional financial advisor and her clients. The value of helping people make sense of their lives. The value of helping people discover, and then articulate, meaningful goals that align with their purpose and things that are important to them. The value of a relationship with someone who is both trusted and who can make a meaningful contribution to clarifying important decisions. The value of a relationship with an expert who can help clients rise far above their own limited view of their journey and not only offer options and alternatives, but implement these in a practical way. The value of holding clients accountable during their journey and providing firmness and discipline when required. They see our value as a leader, a coach, a mentor, a guide, a confidante, an expert who understands the financial terrain through which each client needs to travel.

How we create value – my perspective

My perspective is a composite of my research and the inspired thinking of some of the great advisors I've worked with. You'll note a sprinkle of Sullivan here and a dash of Murray there. My objective is to provide you with ideas and content that will enable you to express your value in your own style. I've taken the approach of considering what a client needs from us and how we are able to respond.

What your client needs and gets when working with you	What you can provide that's of value
Leadership, strategic direction and goal clarification	Few people lead deliberate lives. Those who choose to, through putting a modicum of effort in identifying some objectives and developing a plan to achieve these, experience considerably more success. You are a leader. You are a guide. You will make every effort to understand (and, in many cases, help your client to understand) what they want and then set a course to get it.

What your client needs and gets when working with you	What you can provide that's of value
Empathy, emotional support, perspective, confidence, accountability and behaviour management	Few of life's journeys are smooth rides. Progress to most worthwhile goals – an academic qualification, running a marathon, saving for retirement – will be peppered with potholes and setbacks. Many people choose to fold their cards when the going gets too tough. Many people make inappropriate decisions when under pressure. You are a coach. You are a partner. You are a captain. They will grow weak. They will grow impatient. They will be scared. And then they will become greedy. You will always be there to counsel them, to empower them to make good decisions and then to hold them accountable once a decision is made.
A trusted resource	These times are truly the Golden Age of misinformation. The media, fund managers, companies and governments all have their own agendas. Sometimes they align with the cause of the individual. Often not. You are a trusted resource with the experience and education necessary to cut through the hype and the noise and who can (and will) provide a filtered, unbiased interpretation of events that may affect your clients' goals.

What your client needs and gets when working with you	What you can provide that's of value
An expert	The sophistication behind a financial plan is most often underestimated. This is because financial advice is intangible and its benefits are most often only apparent after the passing of many years. Few clients appreciate the expertise and experience required to assess the terms and conditions of insurance contracts, the quantification of insurance and investment goals and the strategies behind tax and other planning.
	But many trade-offs exist. There are often many permutations to get from today to some future goal. You bring capability to the relationship. You bring options. You bring solutions.
Time saving	Many people complain that they are too busy. But few people respect their time. They are simply not aware of the massive benefits of outsourcing.
	The filing, the research, the compliance and the administration is no longer your client's problem.

What your client needs and gets when working with you	What you can provide that's of value
Framing and simplifying important decisions	Who do you talk to when making important decisions? Do you have the time, knowledge and perspective to make good calls? You provide your clients with a trusted and knowledgeable sounding board. You invest time and effort helping them to carefully consider their most important decisions.
Education and empowerment	Financial literacy is lacking the world over. Your client has an open invitation to ask questions, to gain knowledge and, through a better understanding of what you do, to find deeper conviction in their plan and the demands it makes of them.
Peace of mind, confidence, security	No explanation needed!

What your client needs and gets when working with you	What you can provide that's of value
Monitoring, scorekeeping, course correcting	This world is not suitable for the set-and-forget crowd. A great plan can soon become obsolete if some important assumptions change. Clients tend to believe that the chances of a successful outcome are much higher than they actually are. This is a common bias found in behavioural psychology called "Optimism Bias" (or, in Australia, "She'll be right"). No, she won't be right. This pot needs to be watched. Water needs to be added, it needs to be stirred and the temperature regularly checked. Failure to do so will result in a burnt stew and a threadbare retirement.
Sophisticated questioning, ongoing discovery, ongoing identification of problems and opportunities	Goals change, attitudes change, relationships change. Not only must the plan be monitored (previous point), but the goals and relevancy of the blueprint must be tested. You will bring relevancy and currency to each relationship through sophisticated questioning and ongoing discovery.

What your client needs and gets when working with you	What you can provide that's of value
Proactive investment management	Yes, you also bring investment expertise to the relationship. But not in the way most clients perceive. You will provide a portfolio that delivers the returns required for the goals and objectives contained in your client's plan to be achieved. You will rebalance and ensure appropriate diversification. You will ensure that the client's risk tolerance is respected. But you will not be measured on portfolio returns. This is in the lap of the gods.

A note on proactive investment management

I believe that there is great value to be delivered here but we are not doing so because of a bad habit we picked up years ago and a fear of offending the masters of compliance.

Many client portfolios are constructed on the basis of a risk profile questionnaire and not on the basis of financial modelling. The logic of the risk questionnaire approach is questionable. It suggests that a client has a particular risk profile and that a portfolio with higher risk will cause your client undue angst and may even see them liquidating when their courage fails them in a volatile market. A portfolio with a lower risk than the suggested client profile will see your client lose the extra growth associated with greater risk. I see two major problems here:

1. I don't believe that anyone has a static risk profile. The risks that we are prepared to endure fluctuate as our perception of the likelihood of those risks being realised changes. Take a typical "growth" investor in the years before the Global Financial Crisis. This was a gung-ho type – keen for high exposure to risk assets and maybe even a bit of gearing. Come the GFC and this action hero panics and makes a dash for cash. He didn't really believe when he was asked whether he would be willing to accept a 30% drop in his portfolio (and to which question he quickly answered "yes") that his portfolio would *actually drop by that amount*! Sure you showed him a few graphs of previous bear markets, but it's just not that easy (in fact, nigh impossible) to imagine the feeling, the fear, the panic that is experienced after a market crash. So we ask a series of questions from the safety of our office while the market is behaving itself and somehow we believe we have a basis on which to construct an investment portfolio? I think not. I believe that this is an anachronism from years ago that we should have outgrown – and would have if the compliance masters did not see such value in this charade when it comes to defending against client actions for investment losses.

2. A plan has a goal, an objective. In our world, this goal can be quantified in dollars and cents. We know that we have four variables to work with to enable our client to achieve this goal – the amount of wealth they have accumulated to date (their existing portfolio), the time between now and the goal date, what our

client will contribute between now and this date to their portfolio, and the expected average return of their portfolio between plan date and goal date. The portfolio return is the easiest and most flexible to work with. Through disciplined budgeting and a commitment to delayed gratification, you could get your client to contribute more. This isn't easy for most people. Similarly you could push the target date of the goal further out and give your client's money more time to grow. This may work with a goal such as a trophy asset, but your client will be less flexible with postponing retirement and completely inflexible if their goal is to give their kids a private education in their last two years of school. If we assume that both contributions and period are fixed for most people, what is the chance of successfully achieving the monetary goal if we construct our client's portfolio according to their risk preference rather than the return required in our modelling work? If – and this is often the case in an under-saved Western world – our client needs a return greater than their risk profile allows and we simply invest their funds in a portfolio that aligns with their risk profile, we can almost guarantee that our client will not achieve the outcome for which they sought our advice. This is not delivering value. It is destroying it.

We deliver considerable value by helping our client to understand this dilemma. By pointing out to a conservative couple with young kids that by bunkering down in a fixed deposit there is no chance that their kids will see the inside of a private school.

And we'll have the same conversation with our older retired clients who similarly seek the safety of cash and who have fond dreams of travel and leaving a legacy to their grandchildren.

Financial modelling and working collaboratively with our clients to demonstrate how various trade-offs impact on the final outcome is the guts of professional advice. Helping our clients understand the impact of each variable and then providing them with options is where our value shines through. That's what we mean when we say "I help people make smart decisions about their money."

Final word

The value provided by the professional financial advisor to her client is delivered in two completely different ways. Like all other professions, there is the technical part. In our profession, technical value is captured in the financial plan, the Statement of Advice. To deliver value here the advisor needs to have a deep understanding of the many facets that come together in a plan: the tax and legislative environment, all strategies relevant to the client's situation, and the mechanics of any products required by these strategies. This is the easiest part to articulate.

However, it is the non-technical aspect of financial advice where the most value lies. Our relationship and the value inherent can be more likened to a coach, a psychologist and a mentor. A relationship with a financial advisor is much deeper and more emotional than the relationship we have with our accountant, lawyer or doctor. There is a reason for this – the success of our clients will depend more on the emotional journey they undertake with us than the technical journey. We don't offer our clients a tax return, contract or prescription. We facilitate the identification of worthwhile goals and offer them the mindset to endure the hurdles that each and every person who sets out to achieve a financial goal will endure. The discipline required to stick with the plan, a hand to hold when markets crash, the commitment that delayed gratification always needs, and an informed and trusted partner to clarify their most important decisions. We are like the team at Weight Watchers when we plan, measure and hold our client accountable, and in that way transform our client's life in a way that no other profession can. We are like the private gym instructor that will help our client to find a level of health and fitness they would never have achieved on their own. We are like the psychologist that enables their client to conquer fear and find the peace that would never have been discovered without that relationship.

It is this non-technical aspect that makes our profession difficult to understand and a challenge to communicate. We operate in a market that has yet to fully identify just what it needs from us. And we cannot expect our market to ever appreciate the essence, the purpose, the meaning of financial advice until we ourselves find some consensus around where our value lies.

There are many financial advisors who still doubt that they can make a good living by only providing advice. In Sydney I was told: "You cannot make a good living by providing advice alone. We all need the commission and fees linked to the product." In Adelaide I heard: "I've been in this business for twenty years. It's not about value. It's about disturbing the client enough to make the sale." Henry Ford said many years ago that "Whether you think you can, or you think you can't – you're right." We choose our beliefs. We cling to our beliefs. But we must remember that we can change our beliefs. The beliefs of many advisors will be challenged as we move towards professionalism. Those advisors who strongly believe that the value and the reward lie in the product are going to struggle. Those advisors who resonate with the thinking of Sullivan, Kinder, Bachrach and Murray will have an incredible journey in the professional realm.

In the words of Nick Murray, "Your price is an issue only to the extent that your value is in question".[39]

Key points from this chapter

- Our market holds misconceptions about where the value lies in doing business with us. Many people believe that the role of a financial advisor is to provide the cheapest premium and superior portfolio returns.

- Value is in the eyes of the beholder. We need to help our prospective clients discover how we will bring value to the relationship.

- A financial advisor who has discovered their why – and thus practises with a deep sense of purpose – has personal power that energises the way they talk about value to their clients. Clients don't just hear a narrative. They sense the conviction and certainty behind your promise.

- Dan Sullivan summarises the value we bring to our clients in three words: leadership, relationship and creativity.

- George Kinder and Bill Bachrach see our value in helping people discover worthwhile goals that align to what they consider important.

- Nick Murray also summarises the value we bring to our clients in three words: faith, patience and discipline. His philosophy is based on the vital role that a client's behaviour plays in the outcome they achieve. Nick says that "behaviour is the dominant determinant in real life returns".

(continued)

Key points from this chapter
(continued)

- We should let a client's required return determine the makeup of their portfolio, not their risk profile. Where the two don't match (as is often the case) we need to discuss this with our client and let them choose.
- The value provided by a financial advisor is both technical and emotional. And it's in the emotional (behavioural) part that our contribution has the most value.

Chapter 8:

The DNA of the close

"I see closing techniques as both ineffective and dangerous. I've evidence that they lose much more business than they gain."

Neil Rackham
SPIN Selling

The movie *Glengarry Glen Ross* sees Alec Baldwin deliver one of Hollywood's greatest rants. In an eight-minute tirade, Baldwin lectures a group of underperforming real estate salesman. "A – Always, B – Be, C – Closing. Always be closing!" he screams at the intimidated group. ABC was the cornerstone of sales philosophy for decades. The greatest compliment you could pay a salesperson was describing them as a "great closer". Sales offices had big boards that showed each salesperson's pipeline. "When are you going to close?" the sales manager would ask at every meeting.

Baldwin gets ten out of ten for entertainment. But we have little to learn from him about closing. For the professional financial advisor the art of closing is subtle and respectful. It is both a specific step at the end of the conversation *and* integrated into every part of the conversation.

Before we discuss how to close, let's first reflect on why people don't like being closed. This awareness acts as a backdrop for us to consider the preferred approach for the financial advisor.

People don't like being closed

We live in very emancipated and enlightened times. Whereas our grandparents and perhaps even parents had a deep respect for authority and tended to believe what they were told, today we are much more cynical and much more individual. As a society we tend to suspend judgement and often require firm proof before we are prepared to commit to anything. We have grown up with deceptive politicians, sports fixing, market manipulation and powerful people who don't seem to be held accountable for their behaviour. We have rejected the legal construct of *caveat emptor* – a Latin phrase meaning "let the buyer beware" – a requirement for the purchaser to ensure that what they are buying is right for them. We have flipped this age-old commercial relationship around and now demand that the supplier take the risk of an item not meeting our exact requirements. The consumer rules. The consumer is empowered. And the consumer is now hyper-sensitive to any perception that they are being forced to make a decision that they are not ready to make. Today's consumer will not be manipulated into buying by using yesterday's closing techniques.

There is a nuance here. We are prepared to accept pressure when faced with a small decision. There is no strict definition of what constitutes a "small decision" – this is purely personal. There's every chance that where you are racking your brain over whether to buy brown boots or black boots and the sales attendant says something like, "You really look great in those black boots, why don't I wrap them up for you?", that you won't feel a sense of rising pressure and see this as an unwelcome close. You'll accept this as the normal encouragement that takes place in a typical retail situation. You'll most likely experience a similar response when an enthusiastic waiter suggests a particular item on a menu and closes with, "Why don't you try that? It's one of our most popular dishes." The effect of pressure here is quite positive. It does close the sale. The interesting thing is that you'll respond in one way to pressure when being sold boots and food and in a completely different way when sold a new car, a home renovation or financial advice – purchases requiring a "big decision". When deciding whether to spend $15,000 on a new kitchen, we don't like to be told that, in order to lock in the quote, we'll need to sign the contract now because prices are going up next week. The principle here is that the bigger the sale, the more we want to feel that we've made the call on whether to buy or not.

Neil Rackham neatly sums up this principle with a cheeky example:

"Since the dawn of history, would-be seducers have known that the effect of pressure is negatively related to the size of the decision. The hopeful young man who uses an Alternative Close such as 'Would you prefer that we sit here, or shall we sit over there?' will usually succeed because he's asking for a small decision. However, the classic Alternative Close of 'My place or yours?' has a far lower hit rate because the decision it asks for is much larger."[40]

A final comment about why we should be so wary of closing. Even if we succeed in getting our client to sign up for our services with a classic close, we need to recognise that we have most likely caused some damage by doing so. Research shows that people who believe that they have been pressured into making a decision tend be less satisfied with their decision. There is a psychological term for this called *post-purchase cognitive dissonance*, more widely known as "buyer's remorse". The delivery of financial advice is often a multi-step process that requires ongoing client involvement. Whether it's medicals, requests for documentation, or additional signatures; we need our client to be positive and engaged, not sulky and resistant because they feel that they have been emotionally coerced into something they weren't ready for.

So if we cannot – or should not – close in the traditional sense, how should we close?

The DNA of the close

For the financial advisor, the art of closing is integrated into every part of the conversation. This integration is the key to our success. It is the recognition that we no longer expect the close to be anywhere near as significant as classic sales philosophy suggests. Closing should not be understood as just the final step of a process, but something that takes place during the entire sales process. Let me pull a few themes together from earlier chapters to show how we secure a close during the process, and then I'll address the key parts of the close itself.

Closing during the sales process: the Statement of Intent

The Statement of Intent prepares our client for a close

In Chapter 3 I introduced the concept of framing. Framing enables us to set the agenda without our prospective client feeling disempowered or disrespected. This is important, otherwise we can remain mired at Stage 1 with our prospective client holding tightly to their emotional portcullis. A good, well-crafted Statement of Intent holds great power because it sets expectations for our meeting, particularly around where we believe the meeting should finish. This is, in fact, a trial close in old-school selling, but so professionally communicated that very few would object. It's not dissimilar to the champion pool player who not only concentrates on making his shot, but on ensuring that the cue ball (the white ball used to strike all the other balls, if you're not a snooker fan) lines up perfectly for his next shot.

Closing during the sales process: advancing rather than closing

The concept of an "Advance" helps us establish an achievable outcome (and thus avoid the premature close)

We cannot approach every meeting with the intention of closing. I'll define closing as getting a prospective client to sign a document that authorises the financial advisor to commence the advice process on a commercial basis. In other words, when the client commits to paying for your services. This commitment can take place at different times of the advice process, depending on the advisor's business model. Some advisors are prepared to provide a financial plan and then only seek a client's commitment to execute the plan. Others require a client's commitment prior to developing a plan. The latter is certainly my preferred model, as you'll have gathered by now that I strongly believe that the value provided by the financial advisor is strategic and behavioural and that the implementation of the plan has a far lesser value.

Irrespective of when I believe the commercial relationship is struck, what is important is for each financial advisor to clearly understand when they are, in fact, closing and when they are "Advancing". This awareness takes a lot of pressure off everyone – both advisor and client. The bottom line here is that the professional financial advisor should not be following Baldwin's advice and Always-Be-Closing, but should be following Rackham's guidance and Always-Be-Advancing. As Chapter 3 suggests, we need to enter a meeting knowing what our primary and minimum objectives are. The professional financial advisor understands that walking into each and every meeting with the only objective being to close the client is simply bad business.

We need to appreciate that some meetings are there to Advance the sales process and others to close. To suggest in our Statement of Intent that somehow we expect our client to make a commitment (to engage our services on a fee-paying basis) at the end of the meeting will ensure that we remain stuck in Stage 1. The client's self-preservation warning lights will be blinking bright red. To suggest that we should be in a position to decide on the next step – as I have in the narrative in Chapter 3's example of a Statement of Intent – will be much more acceptable to our prospective client. As this still leaves us in the dark about when we can and should close, here we can rely on the cognitive map.

Closing during the sales process: the cognitive map

The cognitive map tells us when to close

I introduced the cognitive map in Chapter 1. The map explains how people make buying decisions. That there is a definite order to our thinking as we move from the defensive mindset we adopt when meeting someone (who we suspect may want us to do something that is not in our best interest) to making a decision to do business with that person. The map shows us that we *cannot close* until we have responded to the buyer's needs in Stages 1 to 4. The bulk of this book provides the skills, insights and tactics to enable us to progress our client's thinking through each stage. We also understand that the cognitive map may not be a linear process. That we could cause our client to doubt our bona fides just when they are asking for details about a particular strategy (Stage 4). This may result in their mindset scampering back to Stage 1 and thus require us to rebuild our perceived trustworthiness. This could happen where we go through specific product details and our client becomes concerned that our choice of product has more to do with a sales target and is less about their welfare. I'm not suggesting that an advisor with some form of target (which is common in bigger institutions) is not acting in his client's best interests. I'm just providing an example of how a perceived conflict of interest could cause a client's mind to retreat into an earlier stage. We could also find our client's mind leaping forward and missing a stage. Having accepted the need to change their position (Stage 2), your client may seek greater details about your proposed solution (Stage 4). The skipping of Stage 3 may be due to them having already made up their mind that you are the correct person to deal with and can deliver the goods. This would typically occur when a client is referred by someone they deeply trust.

Becoming skilled in the use of the cognitive map helps us decide *when* to close. We understand the journey our client's mind will undertake and we can spot in which stage it rests. We'll know that when our client moves into question mode and seeks details that they are in Stage 4. In Stage 4 you are answering questions with diagrams on your whiteboard. You are pointing out details in marketing and product material. You are modelling with fancy software on your iPad or laptop or desktop. Your client peppers you with questions and you answer each and every one. Some clients may need some encouragement before they find their own questions. Encourage them to do so with a few prompters, "Are you comfortable with the need to reposition your portfolio so that we achieve the required diversification?", "Would you like me to run through the difference between stepped and level premiums?" You'll know when your client is about to move into Stage 5 when you ask them if they have any more questions: "Is there anything else that's not clear? Have you any more questions that you'd like me to answer?" And they answer, "No. I think I understand all the points we have discussed."

By the way, what happens if we move too early and try to close a client whose mind has not reached Stage 5? Easy to answer – they'll raise an objection.

Closing

Your client's mind has reached Stage 5. They have trusted you sufficiently to move to Stage 2. They have recognised that their current position is not acceptable and feel a degree of discomfort and have moved to Stage 3. They consider the effort required to address their subpar position worthwhile and believe that you are the right person to help them – and indeed can help them – and have moved to Stage 4. They have asked many questions about planning strategies and product choices and believe that they are sufficiently informed to make a decision and have moved to Stage 5. You are now in a position to close. You'll do so in three steps:

- The summary
- The question
- The silence

The summary

"Successful salespeople pull the threads together by summarising key points of the discussion before moving to the commitment."

Neil Rackham, *SPIN Selling*

Your client's mind rests in Stage 5. Now is the time to pull the key points of your conversation together. This is not a blow-by-blow summary but a specific focus on two parts of the conversation: your client's objectives and what currently prevents these from being achieved, and the solutions you propose to provide. This should be a very powerful part of your dialogue. By listing one issue after another you enable your client to fully comprehend and appreciate the weakness of their current position and the opportunities they are able to seize. Your client may have considered some or even all of these issues at one time or another. But to hear you talk through them one after another – almost counting them off with your fingers, bang … bang … bang … – magnifies awareness and motivates action. And, while this list of woes (or inspired possibilities) is foremost in your client's mind, you summarise the solutions you've proposed.

The question

"The most natural, and the most effective, way to bring a call to a successful conclusion is to suggest an appropriate next step to the customer."

Neil Rackham, *SPIN Selling*

All that remains is for us to simply ask for agreement to proceed. Here are a couple examples of commonly-used closing questions:

"The next step would be for me to draft a plan that records the outcomes you are looking to achieve and specific details of the solutions I've suggested you consider. Would you like me to get things moving?"

Or simply:

"Are you comfortable to proceed on the basis we've discussed?"

The silence

After we ask our question we remain silent.

The professional sales performance company, Miller Heiman, talks about the "Golden Silence" – a three to four second pause after asking a question. The Golden Silence should definitely be used after the crucial closing question.

Tom Lambert, in his book *The Power of Influence*, is a bit more blunt. He advises we: "Just shut up, smile and wait for them to say 'yes please.'"

Final word

I would be doing a grave disservice if I over-emphasised the enabling skills required to close. Savvy real estate investors have a favourite saying: "Money is made when you buy, not sell." There's a joke about equity investors that goes something like: "What's the definition of a long-term investor? A short-term investor who stuffed up." Both suggest that most of the effort and the thinking should be applied at the beginning, not at the end. That if you have not had a good start to the journey it is very difficult to fix things up at a later stage. This is so absolutely true for the sale of financial advice. Our hard work should be focused on building rapport and trust and then helping our prospective client discover their true financial situation. We should recognise that when we are talking with someone who realises that they have a problem (or an opportunity) that they are motivated to do something about, and who believes that we are the right person to work with, then closing is just a formality.

I introduced Andrew Watt in Chapter 3, one of the most accomplished and successful advisors I have worked with and certainly a prolific closer. Let's give Andrew the final word in this chapter:

"Closing is no longer relevant. The sale will close if value is established earlier on."

Key points from this chapter

- People don't like being closed. For big decisions they want to feel that they've made the call.
- You could coerce people into buying using classic closing techniques, but this can lead to buyer's remorse and damage the relationship.
- Closing is not just a step at the end of the sales process; it should be integrated into every part of the conversation.
- The Statement of Intent helps to close because it communicates to the client that we expect to achieve an outcome at the end of the meeting. The outcome could be an Advance or it could be a close.
- We should not look to close at every meeting. In fact, our objective for most meetings should be an Advance, not a close.
- The cognitive map tells us when we can close. If a client is not in Stage 5 they cannot be closed. They will raise an objection.
- The actual close takes place in three steps: the summary, the question and the silence.

Dawn of a
profession

> *"Let us therefore brace ourselves to
> our duties, and so bear ourselves,
> that if the British Empire and its
> Commonwealth last for a thousand
> years, men will still say, this was their
> finest hour."*
>
> Winston Churchill

We move inexorably towards our finest hour.

Since the birth of our profession in the early 80s, we have struggled with a mixed identity. Do we provide professional advice that, in many cases, is given life through product? Or do we sell products under a thin veneer of professional advice? Our destiny lies on whether we believe the former or the latter.

This is no exaggeration. Our ability to speak with conviction, the firmness with which we present our value and our fees, and our reliance on the quality and performance of product all rest on how we choose to see ourselves. And how we see ourselves, and the words and deeds we choose to communicate our purpose, will strongly influence the perception of others – both our critics and those who we serve.

We move towards our finest hour. The need for professional financial advice should be more obvious today than at any time in our short history.

The emergence of financial advice coincided with the greatest asset bull market the world has yet experienced. Cynically, I might say that financial advice emerged *because* of this bull market – as a sophisticated marketing strategy to capture assets.

The close association of financial advice and portfolio performance created the perception that good financial advice equalled good investment returns and vice versa. The association also cemented the inappropriate fee structure that linked professional fees to the size of the investment portfolio. Many in our profession, and among our clients, still believe that the nexus between reward and returns is the most appropriate fee model. They think this because they hold the belief that good financial advice equates to good portfolio returns.

As a profession we now stand at our crossroads, our moment of truth – do we bunker down, embrace the market's perception of our raison d'être and pray for perpetual bull markets? Or do we reset our dialogue with our market?

Of course it should be the latter. Some will say that I'm not being commercial. That we need to sell product to make a living. That is simply not true. The accounting profession sells no product. Neither do lawyers, nor doctors, architects, sworn appraisers, business consultants, analysts … you name the profession. Yet these professions attract billions of dollars in fees.

We need to reset how we are perceived. We need to rebrand ourselves. We need to clearly communicate exactly where the value lies in doing business with us. And we can do this one conversation at a time.

Now, when we talk to our referral partners and when we talk to our prospective clients and when we talk to friends and family, we must talk about how our world has changed and how our profession has now emerged as the most vital and the most relevant to meet this change.

We must talk about how the days of an easy buck are behind us, and will most likely be behind us for some time. I have no crystal ball, but the massive contribution that ballooning credit played in global aggregate demand has peaked and is now contracting. Every dollar of debt is a dollar spent yesterday that must be repaid tomorrow – or if not repaid then at least serviced. We have been spending tomorrow's income for decades. The mass marketing machine ensures that we are never satisfied. Instead of encouraging the thrift and discipline required to reduce debt (and especially debt growth) to manageable levels, central bankers, politicians and business leaders promote further spending, justifying this as necessary for "growth". When the cost of debt becomes too onerous for even countries to service, interest rates are reduced until, in many cases, they are forced to zero. Savers are smashed. Whereas in the past this would have provoked much higher inflation, global overcapacity, labour wage arbitrage and productivity gains ensure this remains muted (or so we are lead to believe from the statistics provided). Even then we wonder why it was that two decades ago we only needed one breadwinner in a family to live a comfortable life. Then somehow our partner needed to get a part-time job to make ends meet. Quickly that part time work became full time and kids needed to be left at crèche or with grandparents for much of the week. Today the typical household sees both parents working and struggles to "make ends meet". How could this be if inflation were muted for so long? How could it be that governments were able to budget for major infrastructural projects in the past, which seem unaffordable in the present? That state assets need to be sold to fund today's current expenditure? That many of today's projects require finance from public-private partnerships? Tax receipts certainly haven't fallen as a share of Gross Domestic Product.

You don't have to look that carefully to observe that the quality of Western economies is not what it used to be. Earnings patterns have changed. They no longer follow a normal distribution curve, but are now more asymmetric. The middle class is being hollowed out. More and more people rely on some form of state welfare. Future growth will most likely be crimped as debt depresses consumption. Inflation is in the system. Add to this mix the demographic bubble of retiring baby boomers – the mega impact of millions of people moving from contributing to the economy to relying on the work of others in the form of state pensions. Some have accumulated sufficient wealth and are comfortably self-funded for retirement. Most are not and will rely on the state for some or all of their income. Many welfare states just don't have the resources for this and don't have the economic strength to address the shortfall. The final straw is, of course, the advances in medicine and health care which ensures that retirees will live longer and require an even greater share of each country's national budget. We are in a financial terra nullis. Mario Draghi – president of the European Central Bank – is quite right when he observes, "We are in a completely different world".[41]

This is the environment in which the financial advisor is called upon to play a leadership role. The risks of relying on the state to adequately fund a retirement are now unacceptable. We are faced with a new risk that is much more deadly than those we have managed in the past. It is called statutory risk – the risk that the contract between the state and its citizens will be redrafted. On a micro level this has happened in giant corporations like General Motors. On a macro level, take a look at the pruning done to the retirement benefits of many European welfare states. Consider the upward shift of the retirement age in Australia. Be aware that the United States has no retirement fund set aside for its population and has an actuarial deficit (the difference between current funding and discounted contracted future payments) of tens of *trillions* of dollars.

The days of consulting with a financial advisor are no longer optional. Every household needs a financial plan – whether a basic household budget or a multi-strategy blueprint. Every household that can afford the services of a professional financial advisor must have one.

We all need to jettison our "she'll be right" attitude and get more serious about the world we are living in. We need to recognise that the free lunch courtesy of ever-increasing debt is just about over. That the coming austerity *is not an option but a consequence* of how we have chosen to live our lives.

Our profession was never about gathering assets. Our profession was never about selling insurance. Our profession has always been about solving problems and seizing opportunities. To date those problems have been put on hold with ever increasing levels of borrowing. It is now twilight for the throw-money-at-the-problem strategy.

Never before has our society been so beset by financial challenges. Never before have so many people needed the skills and support of the financial advisor.

We move towards our finest hour.

Further Reading

Andrew Sobel and Jerold Panas, *Power Questions*

Dale Carnegie, *How to Win Friends & Influence People*

Dan Sullivan, *The Dan Sullivan Question*

Daniel Goleman, *Emotional Intelligence*

David H. Maister, Charles H. Green & Robert M. Galford, *The Trusted Advisor*

Kenneth H. Blanchard, *The One Minute Manager Meets the Monkey*

Neil Rackham, *SPIN Selling*

Nick Murray, *Behavioural Investment Counselling*

Robert B. Cialdini, *Influence, The Psychology of Persuasion*

Simon Sinek, *Start With Why*

Spencer Johnson, *Who Moved My Cheese?*

Tom Lambert, *The Power of Influence*

Viktor E. Frankl, *Man's Search for Meaning*

Acknowledgements

The journey for this book started many years ago. It would not have begun had my late father, Dr Shlomo Peer, not been such a powerful and influential figure in South Africa's life insurance industry. He had complete belief in the value and importance of insurance as the cornerstone of every person's financial security. He lived with deep purpose, held strong convictions and influenced many. I am but one of his disciples.

I have stepped in and out of corporate life several times. Richard Rasker (then Zurich Financial Services) and Paul Fog (National Australia Bank) were great supportive bosses who gave me the space to discover new ideas and the platforms to share these with many others.

Thank you to all my friends and colleagues with whom I spent hours debating the issues contained in this book over a coffee or glass of good red. I learnt from all of you.

Ours is a very generous community. To the many financial advisors who shared their great thinking, their challenges, their lives with me, thank you.

Thank you to my editors Jeremy Sherman and Jacqui Pretty.

And thank you to my wonderful wife Leanne, and my awesome daughters Jessie and Ruby. Thank you for patiently listening to me express my ideas and insights. I know that it's not edge-of-the-seat stuff, but it's stuff I'm passionate about!

About the Author

Dani Peer has been involved in financial services for over twenty years. He started his professional life in the early 90s as an articled clerk at the accounting firm Arthur Andersen & Co. During his articles he developed a passion for financial planning and successfully wrote the entrance exams to become a Fellow of the Institute of Life and Pension Advisors, South Africa's forerunner to the Certified Financial Planner accreditation.

After practising as a financial advisor, Dani soon discovered that his passion lay in helping other advisors enhance their practices. He has stuck with this theme through periods of self-employment and in corporate careers. He spent several years supporting self-employed practices as National Manager, Practice Management at Zurich Financial Services and through his consultancy The Peer Effect. His next corporate stint saw him turn his attention to the challenges associated with a salaried advisor channel as Head of Advice Development at National Australia Bank Financial Planning.

Throughout Dani's career he has mixed his formal work commitments with teaching and training others. He has encountered wildly differing experiences ranging from the formality of being on the faculty of a large business school to delivering the basics of motivation at a tyre repair shop.

Dani was born in Israel, grew up in South Africa and is now living in Australia. He thinks twice before discussing politics.

Endnotes

1   *The Consultant's Consultant* – June 2005

2   *The Consultant's Consultant* – June 2005

3   *The Power of Influence* by Tom E. Lambert, page 47

4   *The Consultant's Consultant* – June 2005

5   *Power Questions* by Andrew Sobel and Jerold Panas, pages 17 to 22.

6   HBR 1998 "The Necessary Art of Persuasion", Professor Jay A. Conger

7   *Behavioural Investment Consulting* by Nick Murray

8   *How to Win Friends and Influence People* by Dale Carnegie

9   www.psychologytoday.com

10 *SPIN Selling* by Neil Rackham, page 44

11 *SPIN Selling* by Neil Rackham, page 44

12 *How to Win Friends and Influence People* by Dale Carnegie

13 *SPIN Selling* by Neil Rackham, page 69.

14 *SPIN Selling* by Neil Rackham, page 69.

15 *SPIN Selling* by Neil Rackham, page 70.

16 http://www.strategiccoach.com

17 *The Dan Sullivan Question* by Dan Sullivan, pages 29 and 30.

18 *The Dan Sullivan Question* by Dan Sullivan, page 30.

19 *Influence: The Psychology of Persuasion*, Revised Edition, by Robert B. Cialdini, PhD, page 129

20 *Storytelling for business leaders* Participant Workbook by Anecdote Pty Ltd

21 *Sources of Power: How People Make Decisions* by Gary Klein

22 *Storytelling for business leaders* Participant Workbook by Anecdote Pty Ltd

23 Nick Murray Master Class 2007

24 *Behavioural Investment Counselling* by Nick Murray

25 Nick Murray Master Class 2007

26 Nick Murray Master Class 2007

27 Nick Murray Master Class 2007

28 Nick Murray Master Class 2007

29 *Start with Why* by Simon Sinek

30 *The DOS Conversation* (workbook) by Dan Sullivan

31 *The DOS Conversation* (workbook) by Dan Sullivan

32 *The DOS Conversation* (workbook) by Dan Sullivan

33 *The DOS Conversation* (workbook) by Dan Sullivan

34 McAlvany Weekly Commentary, 04 June 2014

35 Bachrach Melbourne tour 2013

36 Nick Murray Master Class 2007

37 Nick Murray Master Class 2007

38 *Behavioural Investment Counselling* by Nick Murray

39 *Behavioural Investment Counselling* by Nick Murray

40 *SPIN Selling* by Neil Rackham, page 30.

41 *The Age*, 06 June 2014

www.ingramcontent.com/pod-product-compliance
Lightning Source LLC
Chambersburg PA
CBHW060409220326
41598CB00023B/3069